Fasting for BREAKTHROUGH and REVIVAL

Fasting for BREAKTHROUGH and REVIVAL

Drs. George and Hazel Hill

Victory International Publishing

Certain words and phrases have been printed in bold print and/or capital letters or underlined for emphasis by the author. However, the content of the verses remain unchanged.

Fasting for Breakthrough and Revival
Copyright © 2006
ISBN No. 978-0-9743265-3-5
By Drs. George and Hazel Hill

Printed in the United States of America

Cover Design:
Blake Schroeder, Intoria.com

Cover Images:
© 2006 JupiterImages Corporation
© 2006 iStockPhoto: Gansovsky Vladislav, Luba Nel

Dedicated to the world wide Victory Family of Churches which were birthed, established and have expanded around the world through much prayer and fasting

Contents

Acknowledgments

We wish to express our deep appreciation to
Capazin Thornton for help in writing, layout, and editing
Blake Schroeder for cover design
Dr. George and Cathy Black for "20 Fasting Tips"
Gary Wondercheck, and Stephen and Marcie-Anna Jasko
for proofreading
Bryan Mehr and Europrint Inc. for printing

Introduction

This book is written to help believers understand the purpose, power and potential of fasting.

Fasting is part of normal New Testament Christianity. Jesus fasted (Luke 4:2). Jesus said to His disciples, *"When you fast..."* not *"if you fast"* (Matthew 6:16). The apostle Paul *"fasted often"* (2 Corinthians 11:27). In his letter to the church at Corinth, Paul advised the married couples not to withhold sexual intimacy from each other, except as they agreed to abstain for a season of fasting and prayer (1 Corinthians 7:5). Through fasting and prayer we are not so much believing for something special, we simply want to see restoration of God's normal!

In the book of Acts it was normal for Christians to boldly and unashamedly pray and worship God. It was normal for the gifts of the Holy Spirit to flow in the lives of the believers with signs and wonders confirming the Word. It was normal for believers to seek God for ways to share the good news of Jesus Christ with the lost and hurting. Christians loving and caring for one another was normal. Generous, cheerful giving was normal. I want to see the restoration of normal New Testament Christianity, where we have a church full of divine happenings all of the time, and I am sure you do too!

We fast and pray because we desire to see God's people and God's work revived. Revival is not something we plan; it is something we seek God for, and fasting is an expression of wholeheartedly seeking God. *"Is this not the fast that I have chosen: to loose the bonds of wickedness, to undue the heavy burdens, to let the oppressed go free, and that you break every yoke?"* (Isaiah 58:6). *"As they ministered to the Lord and fasted the Holy Spirit said..."* (Acts 13:2).

Fasting does not change God, it changes us so we are more able to receive from Him and be used by Him. One Word from God can spark revival and move us into Holy Spirit directed and empowered service. This is what transforms nations and changes the world. I pray this book will give you a healthy appetite for fasting!!!

1

Different Kinds of Fasts

Fasting means to abstain from food and/or drink. Biblical fasting is not merely going without food, but taking the time normally spent preparing and eating food and using that time for spiritual purposes. The person fasting will set aside time to read and meditate on God's Word, to pray and talk to God, and to worship and praise Him.

In both the Old and New Testaments we see several different kinds of fasts: (1) the total or absolute fast, (2) the normal fast, (3) the supernatural fast, and (4) the partial fast.

1. The Total or Absolute Fast

The total or absolute fast is where you have **no food or water for a short period of time, usually for no more than three days**.

As you probably know from science class, the human body is made up of approximately eighty percent water. On a daily basis we can lose quarts of water through perspiration, evaporation, and elimination. We need at least eight glasses of water a day to keep tissues healthy, for organs such as the kidneys and heart to function properly, for healthy blood flow, and for all other metabolic functions of the body.

People can typically go without food for extended periods of time. However, **three days is generally the maximum period of time the human body can go without water**.

Esther, her handmaidens, Mordecai, and the children of Israel went on a total fast to save the Jewish people who were about to be exterminated because of an unrighteous decree (Esther 4:1-16). For three days they abstained from food and water. Because of their fasting and seeking God, a nation was saved from annihilation; the evil Haman, who was behind the hate-filled decree, got his just due on the gallows; and Mordecai, Esther's uncle and mentor, was rightly promoted and honored.

2. The Normal Fast

A normal fast **allows for water, but excludes all food**. This makes it possible to fast up to forty days as Jesus did. The Scriptures tell us that immediately after He was baptized in the Jordan River, and being *full of the Holy Spirit,* He was *led* (literally "driven") by the Spirit into the wilderness where he fasted forty days and forty nights. There, He *"ate nothing, and afterward, when they had ended, He was hungry"* (See Luke 4:1-2). The Scriptures say that Jesus did not eat any food, but they do not say whether or not He drank any water.

A forty-day fast is sometimes called a complete fast because the body passes through three different stages during such a long fast. The first stage is a craving for food, which may last for two to three days. The second phase includes a feeling of weakness and faintness. The third phase is the easiest, as the body grows in strength there is little or no desire for food. This phase ends when hunger returns and the body draws on its own living cells. This usually happens somewhere between twenty-one and forty days.

During the time that Jesus fasted the devil continually tried to entice Him to sin. However, Jesus, full of wisdom and the power of the Holy Spirit, successfully resisted the devil by declaring the precise scripture to neutralize every one of the devil's evil solicitations.

There were three different temptations, and Jesus responded with three different passages of scriptures.

> *Now when the tempter came to Him, he said, "If You are the Son of God, command that these stones become bread."*
>
> *But He answered and said, "It is written, 'Man shall not live by bread alone, but by every word that proceeds from the mouth of God.'" (Matthew 4:3-4)*

***

> *Then the devil took Him up into the holy city, set Him on the pinnacle of the temple, and said to Him, "If You are the Son of God, throw Yourself down. For it is written: 'He shall give His angels charge over you,' and, 'In their hands they shall bear you up, lest you dash your foot against a stone.'"*
>
> *Jesus said to him, "It is written again, 'You shall not tempt the LORD your God.'" (Matthew 4:5-7)*

***

> *Again, the devil took Him up on an exceedingly high mountain, and showed Him all the kingdoms of the world and their glory. And he said to Him, "All these things I will give You if You will fall down and worship me."*
>
> *Then Jesus said to him, "Away with you, Satan! For it is written, 'You shall worship the LORD*

> *your God, and Him only you shall serve.'" (Matthew 4:8-10)*

At this point, the devil left Jesus ("*until a more opportune time*"), and angels came and ministered to Him (Matthew 4:11; Luke 4:13).

James says, "*Therefore, submit to God. Resist the devil and he will flee from you*" (James 4:7). Jesus submitted to God by obeying Him. He resisted the devil by declaring the precise Scripture to nullify each and every temptation.

You can be victorious on a normal fast (water only) up to forty days if you are full of the Holy Spirit and have a good measure of God's Word stored in your heart. Then, when the devil comes to tempt you, you can rely on the Holy Spirit to bring to your remembrance the precise scripture to oppose the devil so that he will flee from you.

3. The Supernatural Fast

A Supernatural fast is where you have no food or water for an extended period of time. You do not choose this fast. It chooses you, that is, the Holy Spirit leads you into it. During the fast, the person is supernaturally sustained.

Moses went on a *supernatural fast*:

> *So he was there with the Lord forty days and forty nights; he neither ate bread nor drank water. And he wrote on the tablets the words of the covenant, the Ten Commandments. (Exodus 34:28)*

Moses was caught up with and sustained by God for forty days and nights. When he came down from the mountain, his face was full of splendor and radiance from having been in the presence of God. The fast that Moses went on was a supernatural fast.

Elijah also went on a supernatural fast for forty days and nights (1 Kings 19:7-8). The only way your body could be sustained in such a fast is if the Holy Spirit leads you into it and sustains you through it.

4. The Partial Fast

Daniel was a man disciplined in the Scriptures and in his lifestyle. He was a man of prayer and fasting. He understood the power of fasting and what it meant from both a natural and a spiritual standpoint.

In Chapters 1 and 9 through 10 of the Book of Daniel, we see Daniel praying and fasting. We will look at Daniel's ten-day partial fast and his twenty-one day partial fast.

Ten-Day Partial Fast (Daniel 1)

Daniel, Hananiah, Mishael, and Azariah were among the children of Israel taken captive by Nebuchadnezzar, king of Babylon. They were captives, but they were privileged captives because they were descendants of kings, from the tribe of Judah. The king of Babylon chose them to be specially trained for three years to learn to serve him in his courts (Daniel 1:3-4). He also appointed them daily portions of food and drink from his table (Daniel 1:5).

Daniel was faced with a problem. He did not want to defile himself by eating the king's delicacies or drinking the king's wine that violated Jewish dietary laws. If Daniel ate of the king's table, he would defile himself spiritually.

Daniel's dilemma was: "If I do not eat, I am going to offend the king and he could kill me. On the other hand, if I do eat, I will offend the King of kings and be cut off from His favor. Which one do I prefer to offend, the king of Babylon, or the King of kings?"

How did Daniel deal with this situation?

> *But Daniel purposed in his heart that he would not defile himself with the portion of the king's delicacies, nor with the wine that he drank; therefore he requested of the chief of the eunuchs*

that he might not defile himself. (Daniel 1:8)

Daniel purposed in his heart that he would not defile himself. Purposing in your heart to think, say, and do the right thing is the first step to victory and favor with God.

Daniel knew the Law of Moses and the health and dietary laws set forth in Leviticus 11. He knew there were animals, insects, poultry, and fish that were good to eat, and animals, insects, poultry, and fish that were bad to eat. One reason for the exclusion of certain foods was to keep the children of Israel healthy. The Bible says of the children of Israel, "*He also brought them out [of Egypt] with silver and gold, and there was none feeble among His tribes*" (Psalm 105:37).

As Christians, we are not obligated to keep the dietary laws of the Old Covenant. Jesus said, "*Not what goes into the mouth defiles a man; but what comes out of the mouth, this defiles a man*" (Matthew 15:11). It is of interest, however, as many doctors and nutritionists will tell you, that the foods set forth in Leviticus 11 as clean are best for your health, while the ones called unclean are the unhealthiest.

Look at what happened after Daniel purposed in his heart that he would not defile himself by eating food considered unclean: "*Now God had brought Daniel into the favor and goodwill of the chief of the eunuchs*" (Daniel 1:9).

God brought Daniel into favor with the chief of the eunuchs—I love that about God! He can bring you and me into favor with the right people in any situation. "*When a man's ways please the LORD, He makes even his enemies to be at peace with him*" (Proverbs 16:7).

The chief of the eunuchs liked Daniel, but he was fearful that he could lose his own life if Daniel and his friends became gaunt and sickly as a result of not getting enough to eat.

> *And the chief of the eunuchs said to Daniel, "I fear my lord the king, who has appointed your food and drink. For why should he see your faces looking*

> *worse than the young men who are your age? Then you would endanger my head before the king."*
>
> *So Daniel said to the steward whom the chief of the eunuchs had set over Daniel, Hananiah, Mishael, and Azariah, "Please test your servants for ten days, and let them give us vegetables to eat and water to drink. Then let our appearance be examined before you, and the appearance of the young men who eat the portion of the king's delicacies; and as you see fit, so deal with your servants."*
>
> *So he consented with them in this matter, and tested them ten days. (Daniel 1:10-14)*

Daniel asked the chief of the eunuchs to give them vegetables and water for ten days, and his request was granted. Guess what happened? *"And at the end of ten days their features appeared better and fatter in flesh than all the young men who ate the portion of the king's delicacies"* (Daniel 1:15). The NIV says, *"At the end of the ten days they looked healthier and better nourished than any of the young men who ate the royal food."*

One of the benefits of fasting is that it will make you healthier. You will get rid of toxins that have accumulated in your body as well as cravings for the wrong kinds of food.

> *Thus the steward took away their portion of delicacies and the wine that they were to drink, and gave them vegetables. As for these four young men, God gave them knowledge and skill in all literature and wisdom; and Daniel had understanding in all visions and dreams. (Daniel 1:16-17)*

This ten-day selected fast proved that God's way is better than man's. Daniel and his friends found favor and increased in knowledge and influence because of this time of consecration. *"And in all matters of wisdom and understanding about which the king examined them, he found them ten times better than all the magicians and astrologers who were in all his realm"* (Daniel 1:20).

The king found Daniel and his friends ten times better, ten times wiser, ten times more knowledgeable, and ten times greater in understanding than everyone else. God gave them supernatural knowledge, wisdom and understanding. He gave them skill in all literature and gave Daniel understanding in all visions and dreams.

These are the last days. The Bible promises us:

> *And it shall come to pass afterward that I will pour out My Spirit on all flesh; your sons and your daughters shall prophesy, your old men shall dream dreams, your young men shall see visions. (Joel 2:28)*

God is revealing things through visions and dreams to His people in these last days. We are going to know about some events before they ever take place. Before the flood came, God divinely warned Noah.

By faith Noah, being divinely warned of things not yet seen, moved with godly fear, prepared an ark for the saving of his household, by which he condemned the world and became heir of the righteousness which is according to faith (Hebrews 11:7).

God directed Noah to prepare an ark to save his life. God knows every tragedy that is going to take place. He knows what business deals to get into and which ones to avoid. He knows how to get you out of a place so that you don't get hurt. God will warn His people before bad things happen.

God divinely warned the wise men to go back to their countries by a different route than they came (Matthew 2:12). He warned Joseph and Mary to flee out of their country and go to Egypt before Herod's slaughter of the innocent Hebrew boys (Matthew 2:13-16). God warned the apostle Paul of persecution to come (Acts 18:9; 21:4). God will warn His people, but we must have spiritual ears attuned to hear.

The week before the December 26, 2004 tsunami caused devastation in eleven nations including Sri Lanka, my friend Mervyn Mediwake was standing on the beach in Sri Lanka and preaching to pastors. God had him in there before the tsunami hit and got him out of there before the devastation occurred.

God has warned me time and time again about different things—where I should be and where I shouldn't. He has frequently kept me out of harm's way.

I assure you, if you make fasting and prayer a part of your life, you will hear God speaking to your heart. You will begin to understand His plan and His purpose for your life. He will guide you through the dark places in life and lead you away from bad situations. Like Daniel, you too can have supernatural knowledge, wisdom, and understanding in visions and dreams.

Twenty-One Day Partial Fast (Daniel 10)

> *In those days I, Daniel, was mourning three full weeks. I ate no pleasant food; no meat or wine came into my mouth till three full weeks were fulfilled. (Daniel 10:2-3)*

Here, Daniel committed to **an extended partial fast to seek God about His will and purpose**.

Daniel ate no pleasant food, that is, no meats and no sweets. He had vegetables and water. We will see later what happened in Daniel's life as a result of this fast.

For many years my wife Hazel and I have gone on a twenty-one day partial fast at the beginning of the year. We drink water and other liquids such as herb tea; and we only eat fruits and vegetables. We have fasted for twenty-one days, as well as for shorter periods, such as ten days or seven days.

Another way you can partially fast is to eat no food, but

drink water and/or other liquids. Fruit and vegetable juices in small quantities, along with lots of water, permit your system to get into a true state of fasting, while providing sufficient strength should you have to work while fasting.

I have personally attested to, experienced and seen amazing results during and after a Daniel fast. I have seen people with stomach problems totally healed, ulcers disappear, and blood disorders healed. I have even heard of people getting back their natural hair color.

Through such fasts, people can be loosed from the bondage of nicotine, alcohol, and drug addiction. Sexual perversions go. Homosexuality will go if one really wants to be delivered, because homosexuality is a work of the flesh. When you fast, you chasten your soul. Works of the flesh and strongholds can be broken so that Christ can live through you.

Abstaining from Other Things

In addition to fasting pleasant food and meat, this is a good time to turn off the television and lay aside reading newspapers and "surfing" the Internet. Simply shut down all the media voices so that you can spend as much time as possible in prayer and in reading and meditating on God's Word.

I am reminded of a certain medical doctor who was going through so much depression he could not continue as a medical doctor; depression was destroying his profession. He ended up flying all over the United States, across Canada and other countries to different clinics trying to find help for the depression he was in. He could not find help anywhere.

He came back to his hometown and remembered the people who had gone through his clinic. He gave them various prescriptions for their conditions. Many of his patients came to our Victory church. They would go back to his clinic a month or two later and would be healthier and stronger.

The Doctor would ask them, "What has happened to you, you look so much better?" And their response was, "Yes, I accepted Jesus as my Lord and Savior and started going to the Victory church."

Finally, after this doctor tried every institution, he came back to town and thought, "I'll try that pastor from the Victory church." I was the last resort. He phoned me and said, "Pastor, I've been having some problems, do you think you can help me?"

So I went over to see him and listened as he explained what his problems were. Then I began to share with him what the answer was, how he needed to make Jesus the Lord of his life, and that his depression would go if He would receive Jesus into his heart and life. He knelt down, received Christ and I broke the spirit of depression off his life. I began to pray for God to touch him, restore him, and minister to him. Then I gave him a prescription: read Philippians 4:6-8:

> *Be anxious for nothing, but in everything by prayer and supplication, with thanksgiving, let your requests be made known to God; and the peace of God, which surpasses all understanding, will guard your hearts and minds through Christ Jesus. Finally, brethren, whatever things are true, whatever things are noble, whatever things are just, whatever things are pure, whatever things are lovely, whatever things are of good report, if there is any virtue and if there is anything praiseworthy – meditate on these things.*

I said, "I want you to memorize this passage of scripture. I want you to get it into your heart. Not only that, I am putting you on a fast from the media: no television, no news, and no newspapers. This is your prescription: memorize these verses, switch off the television, and stop ordering the newspapers for at least a month."

The next morning I received a phone call, just twenty-four hours later, this medical doctor, a brilliant man, said, "I received a miracle. I received a miracle, and I don't believe in miracles. It is God. The depression is gone. I can think straight. I'm back to normal." The following week he came to church and publicly received Christ as Lord and Savior.

Abstaining from the media and replacing that time with God's Word gives God the opportunity to speak to your heart. Some people are simply addicted to all the *bad news.* We have to become addicted to *the Good News.* Take the Gos-pills of: Matthew, Mark, Luke and John. A Gos-pill a day *will* keep the doctor away.

Dr. Jesus' prescription for life and health:

> *My son, give attention to my words; incline your ear to my sayings. Do not let them depart from your eyes; keep them in the midst of your heart; for they are life to those who find them, and health to all their flesh. (Proverbs 4:20-22)*

> *Anxiety in the heart of man causes depression, but a good word makes it glad. (Proverbs 12:25)*

Jesus said, *"It is the Spirit who gives life; the flesh profits nothing. The words that I speak to you are spirit and they are life"* (John 6:63).

God's words are *"spirit"* and they are *"life."* They are *"health"* to all our flesh.

Give it a Rest

We all know that our stomachs need a rest. The stomach, for some people, is the most overworked part of their whole body.

The stomach is at work even when you sleep. If you eat a heavy meal before going to bed, your stomach will work all night trying to digest it. You wake up tired because your stomach has been in labor all night. It is time to give our stomachs a rest.

Set Time aside to Fast and Pray

The ideal would be for us to shut down everything, take off and go to a mountain retreat or some small island to fast, pray, and spend time with the Lord. If you can do this, fantastic! Most people, however, especially those married with children, or single with children, are not able to get away from the responsibilities that accompany having a family. They have to rise early and go to bed late in order to spend quality time with the Lord. The Daniel fast is excellent, because it is the kind of fast that the whole family can participate in and benefit from.

You can read Bible stories to your little ones, or have a Bible study and prayer service together with your older children before your own consecrated time with the Lord. You will also be training them to eat healthy.

Press Toward the Goal

In the natural, we need to stop living to eat, and learn to eat to live. Spiritually, we need to learn to live by every Word that proceeds from the mouth of God; and grow up to the measure of the stature of the fullness of Christ, and do the greater works He commissioned us to do (Matthew 4:4; Ephesians 4:15; John 14:12).

If you will make fasting and prayer a regular part of your lifestyle, you will make tremendous progress spiritually and will find that you are healthier in every respect.

2

Humbling the Soul

When I wept, [and chastened] my soul with fasting, that was to my reproach. (Psalm 69:10)

King David wept and chastened his soul with fasting. Chasten means "to instruct", "to teach" and "to reprove." The number one reason to fast is to humble the soul and break the flesh's power to rule your life.

The soul is the self-conscious part of who we are. It is the part of us that says, "I wish," "I want," "I need," "I feel". It is the part of us that unless reproved, disciplined and rightly instructed will be self-centered, self-justifying and self-defending.

What you feed will flourish, what you starve will die. When you fast, lust begins to die, greed begins to die, covetousness begins to die, unbelief goes, and a rebellious and independent spirit will cease to exist. With fasting, everything outside the will of God loses its pull and attraction.

Have you ever heard anyone say, "Fasting just kills me?" Well, guess what? That is exactly what it is supposed to do. It is supposed to kill, or put an end to, whatever is selfish, critical, or carnal in you. Fasting will teach your soul who really is in control; and your spirit, by the Holy Spirit in you, will rise to that preeminent position.

The Folly of an Uncontrolled Appetite

An uncontrolled appetite will lead to barrenness and spiritual disaster in your life.

Esau sold his birthright for one morsel of food

> *Pursue peace with all people, and holiness, without which no one will see the Lord: looking carefully lest anyone fall short of the grace of God; lest any root of bitterness springing up cause trouble, and by this many become defiled; lest there be any fornicator or profane person like Esau, who for one morsel of food sold his birthright. For you know that afterward, when he wanted to inherit the blessing, he was rejected, for he found no place for repentance, though he sought it diligently with tears. (Hebrews 12:14-17)*

For one morsel of food (some lentil stew) Esau gave up his birthright to his brother Jacob (Genesis 25:34). Jacob wanted Esau's birthright, and he got it because Esau placed more value on carnal things than he did on spiritual things. Because he could not control his appetite he forfeited God's blessings and purpose for his life and brought barrenness to his own soul.

The Scriptures could have read, "The God of Abraham, Isaac and Esau." But Esau gave away his inheritance in exchange for a little instant fleshly gratification. An uncontrolled appetite will always lead to barrenness, poverty and spiritual disaster.

> *Hear, my son, and be wise; and guide your heart in the way. Do not mix with winebibbers, or with gluttonous eaters of meat; for the drunkard and the glutton will come to poverty, and drowsiness will clothe a man with rags. (Proverbs 23:19-21)*

Adam and Eve gave up Paradise for one bite of fruit

In the Garden of Eden, Adam and Eve gave in to the temptations of the devil, and ate of the fruit God told them not to eat. They gave up their innocence, their intimate relationship with the Lord, and their God-given dominion in the earth because of "*the lust of the flesh, the lust of the eyes, and the pride of life*" (1 John 2:16).

The Bible says that because of Adam's sin, sin and death entered the world (Romans 5:12).

People Out of Control

Some people are consumed with thoughts of food. The Bible speaks of people "*whose god is their belly*" (Philippians 3:19). They spend half their lives thinking about what they are going to eat. They eat breakfast and then think about what they will have for a snack. Then while they eat the snack, they think about what to have for lunch. At lunch they think about what to have for dinner. And after dinner, they think about what to have before they go to bed. They are bound by food. They are out of control.

Like a Broken Down City

> *Whoever has no rule over his own spirit is like a city broken down, without walls. (Proverbs 25:28)*

When a city's walls are broken down, it means the enemy can come in and take it. At any given time, the enemy can take control of a person who has no control over his appetites, passions and lusts. These people are vulnerable and can be lured away from church, pulled away from the Word, from worship, and from God's destiny for their lives, all because they lack self-control.

Victory through Christ

Jesus Christ, whom the Scriptures call *the last Adam* (1 Corinthians 15:45) was tempted in every way as we, yet He did not sin (Hebrews 4:15). After fasting forty days and nights in the wilderness Jesus was hungry. The devil came to Him and said, *"If you are the Son of God, command that these stones become bread"* (Matthew 4:3). The devil tried to get Him to respond from His own will, independent of God.

But Jesus answered and said, *"It is written, Man shall not live by bread alone, but by every word that proceeds from the mouth of God"* (Matthew 4:4).

Jesus, by putting more value on spiritual things, won back for us everything that the first Adam lost. Everything was restored because he would not let his appetite or fleshly desires control his life.

> *For if by one man's offence death reigned through the one, much more those who receive abundance of grace and of the gift of righteousness will reign in life through the One, Jesus Christ. (Romans 5:17)*

We have to restrain the flesh or it will dominate us. The apostle Paul said, *"I discipline my body and bring it into subjection, lest, when I have preached to others, I myself should become disqualified"* (1 Corinthians 9:27).

Fasting and prayer are designed to put the spirit man, which was created in righteousness and true holiness, back in control of your life. Fasting and prayer will shut the mouth of the flesh and open the ear of the spirit man to God.

There are some answers to problems in your life you will not receive until you fast and pray. There are some things that will never happen for you unless you fast and pray.

> *This kind can come out by nothing but prayer and fasting. (Mark 9:29)*

Adding fasting to your prayer will give you extra spiritual muscle to press through to your breakthrough.

Through fasting and prayer, we die to ourselves. As we die to ourselves, Jesus becomes more alive in us. The goal of chastening our souls through fasting is to be able to say with fresh conviction, *"I am crucified with Christ, nevertheless I live, yet not I, but Christ lives in me"* (Galatians 2:20).

3

Revelation and Direction

> *That the God of our Lord Jesus Christ, the Father of glory, may give to you the spirit of wisdom and revelation in the knowledge of Him (Ephesians 1:17)*

Once you begin to bring the flesh into subjection to your spirit, God can speak to you more clearly. One Word from God can change your whole life. One Word from God can bring new life to hopeless situations. It can do things in your life that nothing else can.

We need to hear God's voice so that we can understand His purpose, walk in His ways, and become everything we are called to be.

The beginning of the year is a great time to fast and pray, seeking God for guidance and direction. This is why Hazel and I always fast for a season in January of every year. We fast at others times as well, but particularly at the beginning of the year.

We set this time aside to refocus our vision and do an overall evaluation of our lives and ministry. During this time the Lord is faithful to reveal both the problems that need to be addressed and the potential that needs to be pursued.

Then the things that take a lot of time, energy, and money and yet bring forth little fruit can be pruned out of our lives. The pruning of the unproductive practices and counterproductive habits out of our lives gives the extra strength and focus needed to forge ahead in the purposes of God.

The leaders in the early church fasted often. The apostle Paul received confirmation and release to the apostolic ministry while the leaders were praying and fasting.

> *Now in the church that was at Antioch there were certain prophets and teachers: Barnabas, Simeon who was called Niger, Lucius of Cyrene, Manaen who had been brought up with Herod the tetrarch, and Saul. As they ministered to the Lord and fasted, the Holy Spirit said, "Now separate to Me Barnabas and Saul for the work to which I have called them." Then, having fasted and prayed, and laid hands on them, they sent them away. So, being sent out by the Holy Spirit, they went down to Seleucia, and from there they sailed to Cyprus. (Acts 13:1-4)*

The prophets and teachers had been praying, fasting, and worshiping God. In the middle of this time of praise and worship the Holy Spirit spoke, that is, a prophetic word came forth prompted by the Spirit of God. This season of fasting and prayer confirmed and brought release to Paul and Barnabus into their apostolic ministry.

That is what we want—*Holy Spirit directed service,* and then *Holy Spirit empowered service.* This is how we enter into the realm of the miraculous. The supernatural favor of God is released to fulfill His purposes, not ours.

We Want God's Pattern for Building His Church

God has a pattern for building His church. This pattern is like the one God gave Moses for the tabernacle.

> *And let them make Me a sanctuary that I may dwell among them. According to all that I show you, that is, the pattern of the tabernacle and the pattern of all its furnishings, just so you shall make it. (Exodus 25:8-9)*

When Solomon's temple was built, King David acknowledged that God had given him the pattern of all things by the Spirit (1 Chronicles 28:12). The Lord said that Solomon, David's son, would build the temple and not David. However, David, by the Spirit, received the pattern and prepared for the building of the temple with all of his heart, mind, soul, and resources. The temple was a place for the people of God to come together for corporate worship and to hear the Word of the Lord.

There is such a thing as a corporate destiny. You do not have a destiny just by yourself; your destiny is linked with others.

Can you imagine an eyeball having a destiny by itself? Of course not! The eyeball could be the clearest, brightest, most beautiful eyeball, but if it is rolling around on the floor by itself, unconnected to the rest of the body, it is totally useless.

Just as God has a purpose for every part of the natural body, He has a purpose for every part of the Body of Christ. He has set every part in the body as it has pleased Him. He has a purpose for the eyeball, for the leg, the hand, the arm, the feet, the nose, the ears, the kidneys, the heart, the mind, and for every other body part. A healthy body has every part functioning effectively and harmoniously together.

1 Corinthians 12:13 says, *"For by one Spirit we were all baptized into one Body – whether Jews or Greeks, whether slaves or free – and have all been made to drink into one Spirit."* Baptized into the Body means you are baptized into people. The Body of Christ is only going to be built up by that which every joint supplies.

It is important for us all to find our place in the Body so that we can do all that He has called us to do and become everything He has designed us to be. Our God-given destiny is directly linked to finding and fulfilling our responsibility in the Body of Christ.

Look at Daniel 9:1-3:

> *In the first year of Darius the son of Ahasuerus, of the lineage of the Medes, who was made king over the realm of the Chaldeans – In the first year of his reign I, Daniel, understood by the books the number of the years specified by the word of the Lord through Jeremiah the prophet, that He would accomplish seventy years in the desolations of Jerusalem. Then I set my face toward the Lord God to make request by prayer and supplications, with fasting, sackcloth, and ashes. (Daniel 9:1-3)*

As Daniel reads through the Scriptures he sees in the book of Jeremiah that Israel is going to be captive for seventy years and then freedom is going to come. He counts the years and discovers that they are living in the year when Israel should be freed and return back to Jerusalem and to their God.

Daniel found it in the Scriptures, and he knew it was the time when these things should happen. He did not take for granted that these events were automatically going to happen. God would not tell us to pray, *"Your kingdom come, your will be done on earth as it is in heaven"* (Matthew 6:13) if these things occurred independent of our response.

There are some things spoken of in the Word that God

wants to happen on earth, but they are not going to happen unless and until we pray. Of course, there are other things that are going to happen no matter whether we pray or not, because God has predetermined and ordained them in His Sovereign will. However, there are many things He desires to take place that we have to birth spiritually through prayer in order for them to come to pass.

Daniel found in the Scriptures that God wanted the children of Israel released from their captivity in Babylon, and the time was at hand. You too can find from reading the Scriptures what God wants to restore to His church in these last days.

Without a doubt, God wants to restore His church back to full power, which is what I call normal New Testament Christianity like we see in the Book of Acts. The early church was powerful, passionate, and progressive. Therefore, it is time we cry out to the Lord for more than what we have experienced up until now. There is more to Christianity, more to church, more to marriage and the family, and more to the God kind of life than what any of us has or is experiencing. I do not know about you, but I want more. David said, *"As for me, I shall be satisfied when I awake in Your likeness"* (Psalm 17:15).

Jesus promised, *"Most assuredly, I say to you, he who believes in Me, the works that I do he will do also; and greater works than these he will do, because I go to My Father"* (John 14:12). We have to believe and pray that this passage of scripture will become a reality in the church today; that the same power, signs, wonders, miracles and gifts of the Holy Spirit will be made manifest through His people today, so that the church can finish what Jesus started.

Daniel found the answer in the Word. The fact is, many times we should not start to pray until we have searched the Scriptures. The Word will not only provoke us to pray and fast, but it will give direction to our intercession.

Some people do not pray because they never get into the Word. You have to read it until something comes alive in your spirit and you get revelation and understand what God is saying to you about the situation at hand. Daniel's experiences should motivate us all to pray and fast for clearer understanding, guidance, and direction.

Daniel prayed three times a day. Notice what happened while Daniel was still speaking, praying and confessing sin.

> *Yes, while I was speaking in prayer, the man Gabriel, whom I had seen in the vision at the beginning, being caused to fly swiftly, reached me about the time of the evening offering. And he informed me, and talked with me, and said, "O Daniel, I have now come forth to give you skill to understand."* (Daniel 9:21-22)

I am sure we could all do with a little more skill and understanding than what we have right now. There is a price to pay for it. God says, "*He is a rewarder of those who diligently seek him*" (Hebrews 11:6). He rewards those who take Him seriously, but not those who are lazy, careless or disobedient. We have to cry out to Him and say, "God, I am not happy with half-hearted, luke-warm, decaffeinated Christianity. I want the real thing and I will not give you any rest until I fully enter into it."

Look again at verse 22.

> *And he informed me, and talked with me, and said, "O Daniel, I have now come forth to give you skill to understand."*

And then verse 23:

> *At the beginning of your supplications the command went out, and I have come to tell you, for you are greatly beloved; therefore consider the matter, and understand the vision.*

Wow! Here is the archangel Gabriel, who stands in the

presence of God, telling Daniel that he is *"greatly beloved."* God said of Jesus, *"This is My beloved Son, in whom I am well pleased"* (Matthew 3:17). Paul writes that believers are *"beloved of God"* (Romans 1:7).

The angel begins to reveal to Daniel what is going to take place in the future. Part of the Holy Spirit's work in the life of a believer is to show him things to come (John 16:13). We do not have to be ignorant of the future. We do not have to fall into every trap the enemy sets for us. Proverbs 22:3 says, *"A prudent man sees danger and hides himself; but the simple go on, and suffer for it."*

By knowing the Scriptures, you can learn to foresee the good and the evil. *"The Scripture, foreseeing..."* (Galatians 3:8). You will be able to see beyond the present, temporary circumstances. You will be able to see what unbelievers cannot see. You will know what the world cannot know. That means you will be able to do what the world cannot do, and go where the unbelievers cannot go.

When we fast and pray to hear God's voice, He will give us understanding. He will impart wisdom to us so we can receive more favor, be more effective, and do things better than we have ever done before.

God is a God of Purpose

Everything He creates has a purpose. If you do not understand the purpose of something, you will abuse it and misuse it. If you have a gift, and you do not understand its purpose, then you will use it for the wrong reasons, thus misusing and abusing it.

We have to discover the purpose of our local church, God's purpose for our lives in the midst of the local church, and then how it all fits together in God's plan for the universal Body of Christ.

Someone once said, "Many moves of God start in a cave of power and then end up in a cathedral without purpose."

When Hazel and I came to California, we created a cave of power, just the two of us in our little one-bedroom condo, praying and seeking God. Soon God sent people to come alongside us who caught the vision and were willing to sacrifice to see it become a reality. They were willing to give and do whatever it took to get the job done.

It is wonderful to be a part of something from the ground floor up. I feel sorry for people who do not like to be pioneers, because they miss out on all the blessings of creating and building something out of nothing. God is the Creator and we are created in His image. Pioneers experience the creative powers of God flowing through them when they give birth to something that never existed before. It never ceases to amaze me when I see a God-given idea birthed, grow, and accomplish great things for the glory of God.

I do not want my church and the Victory movement that I am a part of to ever stop growing and thus become a cathedral without purpose. We put the purpose God has given us on the back of every bulletin, every magazine, and every piece of literature. By doing so, this helps us to stay focused and never forget the reason why we exist.

The Basic Purpose of a Victory Church

Evangelism

The basic purpose of each Victory church is to reach every available person at every available time by every available means with the gospel of Jesus Christ. Thus, we must receive creative ideas from God to be able to accomplish this.

There are too many backslidden Christians in North America. Many of them have been hurt or offended in church and they are sitting at home doing very little to advance God's Kingdom and usher in the return of Christ. However, God is a God of restoration, and before the return of Christ, I believe North America will experience another Great Awakening.

> *Can he take these burnt stones out of the rubbish and use them again? (Nehemiah 4:2)*

The enemy tried to discourage Nehemiah from rebuilding the temple. Just like today, the enemy would have us to believe that the "stay-at-home group" are just a bunch of burnt Christians—disgruntled, hurt, wounded, offended. Nobody is ever going to be able to use them again. Can **He** take these burnt stones out of the rubbish, clean them off and use them again? **Yes**! **Yes**! **Yes**!

God is the God of the first chance, second chance, third chance, fourth chance, fifth chance, and more, *"His hand is stretched out still"* (Isaiah 9:17). If you are alive, God can use you. He has a purpose for you. If there were no purpose for you, God would not have allowed you to be living at this time.

We need creative strategies for reaching out to the communities, touching the backsliders, and saving the lost. There are many different ways to evangelize, many different kinds of outreaches, and we need the right ones, at the right time for the right people.

Discipleship

The second purpose of every Victory church is discipleship, in which we train and teach people to become like Jesus Christ.

We believe discipleship takes place best in the Small Group setting. We encourage everyone to not only attend the Sunday Celebration Services but to be a part of one of our small groups that we call "Life Groups". There are three main objectives of our Life Groups:

- **Transformational**, life changing, becoming more like Jesus;
- **Relational**, every one finds a friend and discovers their

place on a team;

- **Missional**, every one understands the vision of the church and finds a ministry in the church and a mission to the world.

When these three objectives are being accomplished, the groups continue to go on and grow on. In these Life Group settings, not only are people's needs met, but they also have great opportunity to discover their God-given destiny. Therefore, we need God's creative strategies to more effectively make disciples who will bring glory to the wonderful Name of Jesus.

Mobilization

The third part of our local Victory church vision is mobilization, to activate the army of God.

Every person is called to some ministry. It does not mean that all are apostles, prophets, evangelists, pastors, and teachers. The five-fold ministry equips and trains the saints for the "*work of the ministry*" (Ephesians 4:11-16).

Each person in the church needs to ask, "Where do I fit?" "What has God called me to do to help build up the church?" It is the job of the five-fold ministry to help people to find their place.

Every local church we have, whether located in India, Africa, China, the South Pacific, Central America, Europe, Canada, or the USA, has the same purpose. The local vision might be different. The methodology might be different, but we have the same purpose—to evangelize, disciple, and mobilize. However, we need the blueprint of God for each particular region.

It is the people God sends into a local church who determine what can be done and when it can be done. A project cannot be started just because the pastor has a vision for it. It takes the right vision, and it takes the right people. The people then have to be ready, able and willing to do what God tells them to do. They cannot be sitting on the top shelf. They must be sitting on the edge of their seat ready and available to be used by God.

When God says, "Now is the appointed time, it is time to move," then the people must be prepared, ready, willing, and able to spring into action.

Through prayer and fasting, we can better hear God's voice for revelation, understanding, guidance, and direction so that we can be perfectly positioned in the Body of Christ in order to fulfill our God-given responsibility. Thus, we become everything we were created to be, for the glory of God.

4

An Expression of Wholeheartedness

Fasting is an expression of wholeheartedness in seeking God. We see this exemplified in Daniel 9.

> *In the first year of Darius the son of Ahasuerus, of the lineage of the Medes, who was made king over the realm of the Chaldeans – in the first year of his reign I, Daniel, understood by the books the number of the years specified by the word of the Lord through Jeremiah the prophet, that He would accomplish seventy years in the desolations of Jerusalem. Then I set my face toward the Lord God to make request by prayer and supplications, with fasting, sackcloth, and ashes. (Daniel 9:1-3)*

What provoked Daniel to pray and fast? He was reading a prophecy from the book of Jeremiah. Here is what he read:

> *For thus says the Lord: After seventy years are completed at Babylon, I will visit you and perform My good word toward you, and cause you to return*

> *to this place. (Jeremiah 29:10)*

Daniel then looked at the calendar and found out that this was the year when God was supposed to return Israel back to her own land. Daniel found a passage of scripture full of hope and promise for Israel.

> *For I know the thoughts that I think toward you, says the Lord, thoughts of peace and not of evil, to give you a future and a hope. (Jeremiah 29:11)*

God's thoughts and plans for Israel are for good and not evil, to give Israel a future and a hope. So are His thoughts towards us. There are a lot of people with no hope in this world. God wants to give us a future and a hope. For that to happen we must receive a word from Him.

> *Then you will call upon Me and go and pray to Me, and I will listen to you. And you will seek Me and find Me, when you search for Me with all your heart. (Jeremiah 29:12-13)*

God says to call upon Him and pray, and He will listen. God will hear. And they who seek Him and search for Him with their whole heart will find him.

> *I will be found by you, says the Lord, and I will bring you back from your captivity; I will gather you from all the nations and from all the places where I have driven you, says the Lord, and I will bring you to the place from which I cause you to be carried away captive. (Jeremiah 29:14)*

Daniel's heart must have been pounding with excitement. God promised to gather the children of Israel and bring them out of captivity back to their own land. Daniel did not take for granted that this return would happen automatically. He immediately began to set his face to seek the Lord in prayer and fasting to birth it into existence.

God has good thoughts and plans for every aspect of our lives. Therefore it is our responsibility to seek out His will pertaining to our marriages, work, ministries and finances. He has a good word for you that He wants to watch over and perform in your life.

God says, *"If you will seek Me, you will find Me, if you search for Me with all your heart."* Daniel took seeking God with his whole heart to mean fasting and prayer. Fasting and prayer is an expression of whole-heartedly seeking God.

In Matthew 6, Jesus expounds on three major acts of righteousness: giving, praying and fasting. This passage reveals God's attitude towards these things. It is not *if* you give, *if* you pray or *if* you fast. It is *when* you give, *when* you pray, and *when* you fast. God expects fasting to be a normal and regular practice in the life of a Christian.

My wife fasted and prayed for me for eighteen months before I received Jesus as my Lord and Savior. Every Wednesday she would fast and pray for me, and for a while my behavior got worse! There was a point when it did not look as though I was going to be saved at all. Nevertheless, Hazel continued to fast and pray for me.

During that time, it seemed that everywhere I went I met a Christian. Every time I turned on the television there was somebody preaching the gospel. I went on a brand new job, and the foreman was a Christian; he had bumper stickers all over the back of his truck. I was on a job singing worldly rugby songs and a guy came up and gave me a tract about Jesus.

I do not ever remember meeting a Christian until I was thirty years old. I do not remember meeting one in England, or Africa, or Canada. In fact I do not remember meeting a Christian until my wife began praying and fasting for me. When she prayed and fasted for me it seemed like God surrounded me with Christians, and Christian materials, which helped to bring me to the place where I received Christ into my life and became born again.

God will never overrule your will; but He does know how to get you to the place of being more willing to do His will—just like He did with the prophet Jonah. Life became so miserable for Jonah until he gave in and said, "Okay Lord, I will do what you want me to do." In the end, God wants to bring each of us to the place where He can bless us and bless others through us.

It was through my wife's prayer and fasting that I became born again. The gospel message had little impact on my life, until my wife began seeking God with her whole heart on my behalf. My wife was reading through the book of Acts when she came to Acts 16:31, *"Believe on the Lord Jesus Christ, and you will be saved, you and your household."* Hazel believed this passage of Scripture and prayed and fasted until it became a reality in our house! Praise God for a praying wife.

What have you found in the Scriptures that God wants to do in your life, family, church or nation in these last days? Acts 2:17-18 speaks of some very important things that will take place:

> *And it shall come to pass in the last days, says God, that I will pour out of My Spirit on all flesh; your sons and your daughters shall prophesy, your young men shall see visions, your old men shall dream dreams. And on My menservants and on My maidservants I will pour out My Spirit in those days; and they shall prophesy.*

We must seek the Lord and begin to pray these things into existence, and add times of fasting with it. Remember, fasting is an expression of wholeheartedly seeking Him. The Lord says, *"When you search for me with all your heart, I will be found of you"* (Jeremiah 29:13-14).

Take a moment and pray:

> Lord, I am one of your servants. You said we would be a prophetic people and You would

give us visions and dreams. You also said there would be signs and wonders. We know these are the last days, so we pray that You would cause it to happen now, in Jesus Name.

Lord, you said, *"He who believes in Me, the works that I do he will do also; and greater works than these he will do, because I go to My Father"* (John 14:12). Lord, we see these great prophetic promises in your Word and we will give you no rest, until we see them become a reality upon the face of the earth. We want to see and be a part of the greater works, so that this gospel of the Kingdom will be preached with power in all the world and usher in the soon return of our Lord Jesus Christ! AMEN.

5

Prevent Judgment and Receive Mercy

Justice is getting what you deserve for your sins. Mercy is getting what you do not deserve—God's unmerited favor.

When judgment was about to come on Nineveh, they repented and fasted. God turned His judgment away and instead began to bless them. One hundred twenty thousand people, and even the animals, fasted! From the king to the cow they fasted. God changed His plans, because the people changed their behavior (Jonah 3:4-10).

In the book of Esther, a decree had gone forth to destroy the Jewish people. Then Mordecai encouraged Queen Esther to go in to see the king and petition him for the lives of their people. However, before she did that she fasted, had her handmaidens fast, and told Mordecai to have the people fast. Everyone did a total fast (no food or drink) for three days. As a result God's mercy was extended to the Jewish people and they were saved from annihilation.

In Acts 27, the apostle Paul, along with two hundred seventy-five other people, was on a ship headed for Rome when a great storm arose. The conditions became so bad that all hope of being saved was lost. However, the apostle Paul had been on an extended fast and during that time the Lord spoke to him and said, "*Take heart, for there will be no loss of life among you, but only of the ship*" (Acts 27:22). Paul believed God, and the crew believed Paul and listened to his counsel. From that time they all fasted for another fourteen days.

When the ship finally sank, not one soul was lost. It happened just the way the angel of the Lord said it would. God even used the shipwreck to reach the entire population on the Island of Malta with the gospel. It is amazing what can be accomplished through fasting and prayer. The Lord can make a way where there is no way; He can turn hopeless situations around and bring victory!

During a personal fast, things God wants us to deal with in our lives come to the surface. When you are distant from the Lord, you can do and say things that are not right and never feel convicted about them because your conscience has become desensitized. But when you pray and fast, and draw near to God, He will draw near to you. It is in God's presence that you suddenly become aware of the condition of your own heart.

Things that never bothered you before start to trouble you, like the words you speak, and the way in which you speak them. You begin to realize when your words wound others, exalt yourself, or contradict God's Word. You understand how the prophet Isaiah felt when he came into the presence of God and said: "*Woe is me, for I am undone! Because I am a man of unclean lips, and I dwell in the midst of a people of unclean lips; for my eyes have seen the King, the Lord of hosts*" (Isaiah 6:5). The prophet Isaiah was the most spiritually qualified leader of his day, yet he was rendered unfit, until his guilt was taken away and atonement made for his sins.

Repentance is not a one-time thing; it is a regular part of our Christian life as we are changed from glory to glory into the image of Christ. In our local church we partake of the communion elements the first Sunday of each month. This is a special time when we come into communion (or intimacy) with our God, who is described by the angels as *"Holy, holy, holy"* (Isaiah 6:3; Revelation 4:8). It is impossible to come into the presence of a Holy God without feeling your need for repentance and cleansing. Thus, before we partake of the communion elements we are told to examine ourselves, and judge ourselves so that we are not judged and chastened by the Lord. The Bible says that because of partaking of communion in an unworthy manner, many are *weak* and *sick,* and many *sleep* or *die* among us (1 Corinthians 11:28-32).

When your heart is pure before the Lord you can pray and fast to prevent God's judgment, and instead invoke His mercy. Scripture promises: *"He will even deliver one who is not innocent; yes, he will be delivered by the purity of your hands"* (Job 22:30).

Take a moment to examine yourself. Psalm 139:23-24 says:

> *Search me, O God, and know my heart; try me, and know my anxieties; and see if there is any wicked way in me, and lead me in the way everlasting.*

Ask the Lord to show you any wicked way in you. As things come to your mind, deal with them. Forgive others and ask the Lord to forgive you. Then humble yourself and allow the Holy Spirit to cleanse you and restore you to right fellowship with Him and others.

1 John 1:9 says: *"If we confess our sins, He is faithful and just to forgive us our sins and to cleanse us from all unrighteousness."*

The Lord is faithful to forgive us and cleanse us when we repent. But even beyond that, we can also be a part of bringing mercy and deliverance to others. Thank God for His great mercy and loving-kindness.

6

Prepare Yourself for Battle

If you are going to accomplish anything significant for God you are going to encounter opposition. There will be battles you have to fight to overcome the devil and the flesh in order to experience the promises of God and advance the kingdom of God.

When the twelve spies went into the Promise Land, what did they see? They saw all the blessings and the benefits. They also saw the opposition, the giants, the walled cities; consequently, ten of the twelve spies were greatly disheartened.

Joshua and Caleb had a different spirit. They kept focused on all the blessings, benefits and promises of God; therefore, they were willing to fight. They prepared themselves for battle and had faith that since God was with them they would win.

Jesus Began Ministry with a Forty-Day Fast

> *Then Jesus, being filled with the Holy Spirit, returned from the Jordan and was led by the Spirit into the wilderness, being tempted for forty days by*

> *the devil. And in those days He ate nothing, and afterward, when they had ended, He was hungry. (Luke 4:1-2)*

Notice that Jesus did not hunger during the fast; he hungered after the fast. If you have ever been on an extended fast you know that after a while you lose the desire to eat at all. There is a point where you feel as though you could fast forever.

However, when your appetite returns and you begin to hunger, that is the time you must eat something. If you do not eat, the body will begin to feed on its own living cells and starvation begins to set in. The hunger pangs are a signal that it is time to eat. Notice that, "*When the devil had ended all the temptation, he departed from him for a season*" (Luke 4:13 KJV). You must realize the devil will come to attack you at various seasons.

- ♦ He will attack you right after you have experienced a great victory, so stay on guard.
- ♦ He will attack you at your weakest point. Know your weaknesses and protect against them.
- ♦ He will try to wear you out so he can wipe you out. Make time in your busy schedule for rest and refreshing in the presence of the Lord.

This is why you have to "*watch and pray*" (Matthew 26:41), keep yourself spiritually strong, and stay covered with the whole armor of God (Ephesians 6:12). You must be especially skillful with the Sword of the Spirit, which is the Word of God (Ephesians 6:17).

> *It is written, Man shall not live by bread alone, but by every word that proceeds from the mouth of God. (Matthew 4:4)*

The weapon that Jesus used against the devil's temptations

and tests was the Word of God.

Living in the Power of the Spirit

Jesus was filled with the Holy Spirit and led by the Spirit into the wilderness to be tempted and tested by the devil (Luke 4:1-2). Then after successfully resisting all temptation, "*Jesus returned in the power of the Spirit to Galilee, and news of Him went out through all the surrounding region*" (Luke 4:14).

Living in the power of the Spirit means being "under the control" of the Holy Ghost. This is a whole new level of life in the Spirit. It is one thing to be filled with the Holy Spirit, but when you are under His control, you operate at a greater level of power and anointing.

We are to be led by the Spirit—not by our heads, not by our bellies, our feelings, our subjective and objective reasoning, nor by our circumstances. God says to be led by, or under the control of, the Holy Spirit, "*For as many as are led by the Spirit of God, these are* [fully matured] *sons of God*" (Romans 8:14).

This level of living requires that we chasten our souls and be emptied of self, until "*it is no longer I who lives but Christ who lives in me*" (Galatians 2:20). It is at this stage that God can use you more powerfully than He has ever used you before.

Look at Luke 4:18:

> *The Spirit of the Lord is upon Me, because He has anointed Me...*

There is an **anointing within** to bring you to the truth and change you personally (1 John 2:27), and there is another **anointing that comes upon you** to enable you to minister to and help other people (Acts 1:8).

Notice the Spirit anoints for a purpose.

> *...He has anointed Me to preach the gospel to the poor; He has sent Me to heal the brokenhearted, to proclaim liberty to the captives and recovery of*

> *sight to the blind, to set at liberty those who are oppressed; to proclaim the acceptable year of the Lord. (Luke 4:18-19)*

When the Spirit of the Lord is upon you, you receive power for a specific assignment God has for you. There is no lack of power with God. Oftentimes what we lack is an understanding of God's purpose. God always anoints you for a purpose.

Instead of praying for God to move, we should pray for His church to move! We should pray for every member of the Body of Christ to discover and operate in his or her function in the corporate Body. When the church–with every joint supplying–begins to go forth in line with God's purpose, then there is provision, protection and power available to fulfill God's assignment.

You must remember, however, that even though you are vital to God's purpose, it is not about you. It is about His kingdom, His will, and His work.

To find that place of purpose, like Jesus we must begin our ministry to others with prayer and fasting.

The Apostle Paul Began Ministry with a Fast

In Acts 9, we read about the conversion of Saul of Tarsus on the road to Damascus. Suddenly a great light from heaven blinded him, and he fell to the ground.

And he heard a voice saying to him, *"Saul, Saul, why are you persecuting Me?"*

Saul asked, *"Who are you, Lord?"*

And the Lord said, *"I am Jesus, whom you are persecuting."*

Trembling and astonished Saul asked, *"Lord, what do you want me to do?"*

And the Lord said, *"Arise, and go into the city, and you will be told what you must do."*

And Saul was blinded three days and neither ate nor drank (see Acts 9:1-9).

Meanwhile, God spoke to a Christian named Ananais. God needed somebody to minister healing and the baptism of the Holy Spirit to Saul. Ananais was attentive to God's voice. Ananais was thus ready and prepared to be used of God.

We all know that Saul, whose name was later changed to Paul, became the great apostle to the gentiles. He wrote two-thirds of the New Testament under the anointing of the Holy Spirit. Notice that Paul's salvation partially resulted because of the sensitivity, consecration, availability, and obedience of a believer named Ananais!

God is Sovereign; nevertheless, He chooses to use people as co-laborers with Him. He uses people who have laid down their desires and taken up His. He uses people who have allowed Christ to live and function through them.

Christ wants your hands to be His hands, your heart to be His heart, your body to be His body. He wants to flow in you and through you to a world that is hurting and needy.

Prepare to Win

We must be prepared for life's battles because temptations, tests and trials will come. God says when they come, "*Count it all joy...knowing that the trying of your faith works patience*" (James 1:2-3). Glory to God! Let patience have her perfect work!

It is more important to have the will to prepare to win than it is to have the will to win. As in athletics, the team that has practiced, trained, and is disciplined is the one that is most likely to win—all other things being equal.

How much do you want to win? How much do you want to see your family saved? How much do you want freedom? How much do you want to see revival and the church become a powerhouse where you live and throughout the world? How much do you want it? Do you want it enough to miss a meal?

My wife wanted me to know Jesus and become born again so much that she prayed and fasted for me—for a year and a half. I want direction for the Victory Church Movement enough to lay aside some of the things I enjoy. I like coffee. However, I do not drink coffee during my fast, because I do not want to be under control of a cup of coffee. I do not want to be under the control of anything but the Holy Ghost and the Word of God.

A cup of coffee is not going to control me. A T-bone steak, bacon and eggs, or fish and chips are not going to control me.

Why? Because I realize I am in a battle, and I want to win.

Are You Buffeting or Buf-faying?

The apostle Paul continually faced battles and opposition. What did he do? He disciplined his body by fasting often, because he wanted to win the race.

> *Do you not know that those who run in a race all run, but one receives the prize? Run in such a way that you may obtain it. And everyone who competes for the prize is temperate in all things. Now they do it to obtain a perishable crown, but we for an imperishable crown. Therefore I run thus: not with uncertainty. Thus I fight: not as one who beats the air. But I discipline my body and bring it into subjection, lest, when I have preached to others, I myself should become disqualified. (1 Corinthians 9: 24-27)*

Paul is talking about the man on the inside, the spiritual man, being in control. "*I discipline my body*" (verse 27). I subdue my body and bring it under control, in subjection to my spirit man. I buffet my body, not "buf-fay" it.

We must discipline our bodies so our bodies do not control the way we live. Remember, an uncontrolled appetite leads to spiritual disaster and barrenness.

> *Woe to you, O land, when your king is a child, and your princes feast in the morning! Blessed are you, O land, when your king is the son of nobles, and your princes feast at the proper time – for strength and not for drunkenness! (Ecclesiastes 10:16-17)*

Did you know it is possible to get drunk on food? Too much food can bring you to the place where you do not think right; the blood that should be in your brain is in your stomach.

I never have a big meal before I preach, even if I am preaching at a banquet. I eat very light if I eat at all; because I know that food will slow me down and make me dull and sluggish. As a result, I will not be able to preach with the sensitivity to the Spirit that I need.

There are many benefits, blessings, and breakthroughs you will receive as a result of fasting. The key to will power is want power. When you can see the benefits of it, then you will want to do it. People do what brings rewards. I pray that you will acquire a healthy appetite for fasting!

An uncontrolled appetite will steal your prosperity, promotion, and every good thing God has designed for you.

> *But take heed to yourselves, lest your hearts be weighed down with carousing, drunkenness, and cares of this life, and that Day come on you unexpectedly, for it will come as a snare on all those who dwell on the face of the whole earth. (Luke 21:34-35)*

Carousing can include "buf-faying" your body, or over-eating continually.

If you put too much of a charge into the battery of your car, the lead plates inside of it buckle and short circuit. Then no power will come out of your battery because it shuts down and the power is dissipated on the inside.

Likewise, too much food interferes with your spiritual reception. It can dull your sense of hearing God's voice. And then no power comes out of your life.

If we are so wrapped up with self and the flesh, we will not be prepared for the battles and temptations that come along. When you indulge the flesh, the flesh loves it. The next thing you know you are out of control and out of God's will for your life.

> *Watch therefore, and pray always that you may be counted worthy to escape all these things that will come to pass, and to stand before the Son of Man. (Matthew 21:36)*

There are a lot of evil things coming upon the face of the earth. We want to be able to hear God's voice and avoid as many of them as is possible. The Bible says, "*The prudent foresees the evil and avoids it, but the foolish pass on and are punished*" (Proverbs 22:3).

Every one of us has blind spots. That is why we need people around us to help. We need people to hold us accountable when we act soulish or contrary to God's Word. We need people with whom we can share our needs and weaknesses and who will pray with and for us. This is one reason why we all need to belong to a good local church, and develop strong relationships with people of "*like precious faith*" (2 Peter 1:1).

In His earthly ministry, Jesus Christ was given the Spirit without measure (John 3:34). Jesus fasted. The great apostle Paul was given "*abundance of revelations*" (2 Corinthians 12:7), from which He wrote two-thirds of the New Testament. Paul fasted often (2 Corinthians 11:27).

If the greatest people in the New Testament fasted for increased spiritual power, then so should we!!!

7

Breaking Demonic Strongholds

Is this not the fast that I have chosen: To loose the bonds of wickedness, to undo the heavy burdens, to let the oppressed go free, and that you break every yoke? (Isaiah 58:6)

And I will give you the keys of the kingdom of heaven, and whatever you bind on earth will be bound in heaven, and whatever you loose on earth will be loosed in heaven. (Matthew 16:19)

I was visiting a church in Canada recently and a woman came up to me and said, "Pastor George, you prayed for me two years ago. I had epilepsy. Every week I was thrown into a grand mal seizure and I was on all kinds of pills. I came to church on Sunday and at the end of the service and you prayed for me." She said, "I was healed that same week and have never had another epileptic seizure. Glory to God!"

Therefore if the Son makes you free, you shall be

free indeed. (John 8:36)

God wants us to be free from worry, fear, pride, addictions, and anything else that would stop us from doing what God wants us to do. Freedom is not doing whatever you want to do. Freedom is having the power to do what you know is right; if you do not have the power to do what is right, then you are not free. If you are not free to obey God's word, then you are not free. If you are not free to go where God tells you to go and do what He tells you to do, you are bound.

God wants his people to be free indeed. How can you set someone else free if you are bound yourself? We have to experience freedom first, and then we can minister life and blessing and freedom to others with confidence and supernatural boldness.

Daniel's Twenty-One Day Partial Fast—A Study in Spiritual Warfare

There is no greater example in the Old Testament concerning spiritual warfare than Daniel 10. We see demons at work to oppose the plan of God and to destroy the people of God. At the same time, we see angels working to fulfill the purpose of God and strengthen the people of God so that they could do their part.

> *In those days I, Daniel, was mourning three full weeks. I ate no pleasant food, no meat or wine came into my mouth, nor did I anoint myself at all, till three whole weeks were fulfilled. (Daniel 10:2-3)*

Daniel fasted and humbled himself for twenty-one days. Thus, look what happened at the end of the fast:

> *Suddenly, a hand touched me, which made me tremble on my knees and on the palms of my hands. And he said to me, "O Daniel, man greatly beloved, understand the words that I speak to you, and stand*

upright, for I have now been sent to you." While he was speaking this word to me, I stood trembling. Then he said to me, "Do not fear, Daniel, for from the first day that you set your heart to understand, and to humble yourself before your God, your words were heard; and I have come because of your words. But the prince of the kingdom of Persia withstood me twenty-one days; and behold, Michael, one of the chief princes, came to help me, for I had been left alone there with the kings of Persia. Now I have come to make you understand what will happen to your people in the latter days, for the vision refers to many days yet to come." (Daniel 10:10-14)

Daniel set his heart to understand

You have to set your heart to understand if you want revelation, restoration, breakthrough, and revival.

Daniel humbled himself

From the first day, we need to set our hearts to understand the word of the Lord. Then we must humble ourselves and surrender our will to the Lord. One of the hardest things to do is surrender your will to another, but we must come to the place where we can say, *"Father, not my will, but Thy will be done"* (Matthew 26:39).

The purpose of fasting is not to try to twist God's arm to change Him. In Malachi 3:6 God says, *"I am the Lord, I change not."*

We are the ones who must change to come into agreement with Him, not the other way around. Fasting helps us to die to self and focus on the Big God we serve, who can turn every problem into an opportunity to advance.

We know that in the last days two opposing things are going to happen: on the one hand, there is going to be great revival; on the other hand, there is going to be a great falling away from the faith. You must purpose in your heart, that you are going to be a part of the great revival, not part of the falling away.

You must be able to deal with hurt and offenses and things that may seem unfair. You must be resilient, able to get up, get over it, and get on with what God wants you to do. You must know the Word of God in your head, believe it in your heart, and stand on it in the face of contradictory circumstances. The apostle John said, *"I have written to you young men, because you are strong, and the word of God abides in you, and you have overcome the wicked one"* (1John 2:14).

Daniel set his heart to understand, and he humbled himself. The angel said, *"Your words were heard, and I have come because of your words"* (Daniel 10:12).

Daniel kept God's Word in his mouth

> *For verily I say unto you, That whosoever shall say unto this mountain, Be thou removed, and be thou cast into the sea; and shall not doubt in his heart, but shall believe that those things which he saith shall come to pass; he shall have whatsoever he saith. (Mark 11:23, KJV)*

> *You will also declare a thing, and it will be established for you… (Job 22:28)*

While Daniel was on the earth praying and fasting for twenty-one days, something was happening in the heavens. On the first day of Daniel's supplications Gabriel, God's messenger angel, was dispatched to bring Daniel the answer. He was sent to Daniel because of the words that he spoke in prayer.

However, there was a battle that went on in the heavens. The Prince of Persia, a devilish, ruling spirit over Persia, actually hindered Gabriel from getting to Daniel with God's message. On the twenty-first day he was able to break through because Michael, the warring archangel of God, came to his aid and defeated the Prince of Persia.

Look at Daniel 10, verses 18 and 19:

> *Then again, the one having the likeness of a man touched me and strengthened me. And he said, "O man greatly beloved, fear not! Peace be to you; be strong, yes, be strong!" So when he spoke to me I was strengthened, and said, "Let my lord speak, for you have strengthened me."*

How we need to be touched by the Lord and strengthened when we are in a weakened state. I think of that old hymn, "Oh, He touched me, and oh the joy that floods my soul."

God's touch strengthens us. God's Word gives us courage and hope. God's messengers exhort, edify and encourage us. We just have to stay connected to our source of supply through prayer, the Word and Christian fellowship.

A word from God was sent to Daniel both during and right after his twenty-one day fast. The angel Gabriel spoke to Daniel:

> *Then he said, "Do you know why I have come to you? And now I must return to fight with the prince of Persia; and when I have gone forth, indeed the prince of Greece will come." (Daniel 10:20)*

The Battle in the Heavens

A lot of Christians have a peacetime mentality. This is not a time of peace, it is a time of war, and there will be no lasting peace until the Prince of Peace returns. You are in a battle whether you like it or not, and you are going to have to learn how to put on the whole armor of God and fight the good fight of faith (1 Timothy 6:12).

There is no such thing as a peaceful co-existence between

the Kingdom of God and the kingdom of darkness. Every battle won or lost on earth is first won or lost in the heavens.

The Power of Binding and Loosing

We have to remember that we do not war against flesh and blood. One of the chief culprits behind all the hatred, murder and war in the Middle East is the Prince of Persia, the same ruling evil spirit that was over that region in Daniel's day.

In Matthew 16:19, Jesus gave us the keys of the Kingdom of heaven: *"Whatever you bind on earth shall be bound in heaven and whatever you loose on earth shall be loosed in heaven."*

Daniel is loosing things in heaven and he is binding things in heaven. He is loosing Gabriel and Michael and a whole band of angels, and he is binding the demon forces.

Your obedience to God's Word binds demons and looses angels and archangels; your disobedience binds the angels and looses demons.

So what do you want loosed in your life? Is it demons, spirits of poverty, sickness, perversion, and other unclean spirits? Or do you want the angels of heaven and blessing? We all have a choice. It comes back to hearing God's voice and obeying what God says.

Heaven Helps Us When We Are On God's Side

> *And it came to pass, when Joshua was by Jericho, that he lifted his eyes and looked, and behold, a Man stood opposite him with His sword drawn in His hand. And Joshua went to Him and said to Him, "Are You for us or for our adversaries?" So He said, "No, but as Commander of the army of the LORD I have now come." And Joshua fell on his face to the earth and worshiped, and said to*

Him, "What does my Lord say to His servant?" (Joshua 5:13-14)

Joshua was going out to fight against Jericho. The Captain of the Lord's Host appeared to him. Joshua had his sword drawn. He said, "*Are you for us or for our adversaries*?" The angel said, "*No,* [I am not for you or against you], "*but as Commander of the army of the Lord I have now come.*"

The angel was saying, you are asking the wrong question, Joshua. It is not whose side I am on; it is whose side are you on? I am here to help you kill the enemy if you are on the Lord's side, or to stand against you if you are not on the Lord's side. Which do you want?

Sometimes we ask the wrong questions. It is not "Whose side God is on." It is, "Whose side are we on." Fasting and prayer will bring us to the place where doing God's will becomes our principal focus.

2 Chronicles 18 describes a conference in heaven deciding how a battle on earth would turn out. King Jehoshaphat, a good king, linked up with a bad king, King Ahab of Israel, and the Assyrians came down to attack them. Ahab wanted the King of Judah to join in with him and called on the prophets to prophesy. They all said, "*Go up to Ramoth Gilead and prosper, for the Lord will deliver it into the king's hand*" (2 Chronicles 18:5).

Jehoshaphat said, "*Is there not still a prophet of the LORD here, that we may inquire of Him?*" So the king of Israel said to Jehoshaphat, "*There is still one man by whom we may inquire of the LORD; but I hate him, because he never prophesies good concerning me, but always evil. He is Micaiah the son of Imla*" (2 Chronicles 18:6-7).

King Jehoshaphat said, "*Let not the king say such things!*" Then the prophet Micaiah was brought quickly for an audience with the kings. Initially when he came he prophesied nice prophecies the same as the other four hundred false prophets.

King Ahab rebuked him and told to him tell the truth. Then

Micaiah said, *"I saw all Israel scattered on the mountains, as sheep that have no shepherd." And the LORD said, "These have no master. Let each return to his house in peace"* (2 Chronicles 18:16).

King Ahab got mad and said, *"Didn't I tell you he would not prophesy good concerning me, but evil?"*

Micaiah went on to say, *"I saw the Lord sitting on His throne, and all the host of heaven were standing on His right hand and His left. And the Lord said, "Who will persuade Ahab king of Israel to go up, that he may fall at Ramoth Gilead?"* (2 Chronicles 18:18-19)

Then a spirit came forward and stood before the Lord and said, *"I will persuade him."*

The Lord said to him, *"In what way?"*

> *So he said, "I will go out and be a lying spirit in the mouth of all his prophets." And the Lord said, "You shall persuade him and also prevail; go out and do so." (2 Chronicles 18:21)*

And he went down and became a lying spirit in the mouth of Ahab's prophets.

Micaiah told the king all of this, and that the Lord had declared disaster for Ahab. One of Ahab's prophets slapped Micaiah for speaking these words. Then King Ahab said, *"Put this fellow in prison and feed him the bread and water of affliction until I return in peace"* (2 Chronicles 18:26).

But Micaiah said, *"If you ever return in peace, the Lord has not spoken by me"* (2 Chronicles 18:27).

So King Ahab went into battle with King Jehoshaphat of Judah. Jehoshaphat had all his royal robes on. King Ahab disguised himself as an ordinary warrior and drove his chariot among the troops.

The Syrians were all looking for the king of Israel clothed in royal garb. It was King Ahab they wanted to kill, but they couldn't find him. At first they thought the King of Judah was him. When they saw it was King Jehoshaphat and not King Ahab, they left King Jehoshaphat alone and kept looking for

King Ahab.

The story goes on to say that, by happenstance, an archer put an arrow in his bow and fired it up into the air. When it came down, it smote Ahab right between the harness, just in the area that was not protected by his armor, and he died.

What an account! The important thing to notice is that the outcome of that battle was determined by a conference that went on in heaven.

Thus we look at the fighting in the Middle East today; it is not the politicians or the soldiers who will determine the outcome of these battles. The outcome will be determined by what happens in the heavens through our prayers and obedience.

Lord, Open Our Eyes

If the believer's eyes were opened they would see angels in the midst of His blood-bought Church because the angel of the Lord encamps around those who fear Him (Psalm 34:7).

In 2 Kings 6, when the Syrian army surrounded Elisha and his servant, Elisha was not bothered at all. His servant got nervous, and said, *"Alas, my master! What shall we do?"*

So Elisha answered, *"Do not fear, for those who are with us are more than those who are with them." And Elisha prayed, and said," Lord, I pray, open his eyes that he may see"* (1Kings 6:15-17).

When the servant's spiritual eyes were opened, he saw that the mountain was full of horses and chariots of fire all around. He got a glimpse into the spiritual realm and saw the mighty forces of God coming to the aid of Elisha. Glory to God! There is more with us than there is with them! If God is for you, who can be against you?

Defeating the Biggest Enemy

> *Now Amalek came and fought with Israel in Rephidim. And Moses said to Joshua, "Choose us*

some men and go out, fight with Amalek. Tomorrow I will stand on the top of the hill with the rod of God in my hand." So Joshua did as Moses said to him, and fought with Amalek. And Moses, Aaron, and Hur went up to the top of the hill. And so it was, when Moses held up his hand, that Israel prevailed; and when he let down his hand, Amalek prevailed. But Moses' hands became heavy; so they took a stone and put it under him, and he sat on it. And Aaron and Hur supported his hands, one on one side, and the other on the other side; and his hands were steady until the going down of the sun. So Joshua defeated Amalek and his people with the edge of the sword. Then the Lord said to Moses, "Write this for a memorial in the book and recount it in the hearing of Joshua, that I will utterly blot out the remembrance of Amalek from under heaven." And Moses built an altar and called its name, Jehovah Nissi [The-Lord-Is-My-Banner; The Lord is My Victory] for he said 'because the Lord has sworn: the Lord will have war with Amalek from generation to generation." (Exodus 17:8-18)

The name Amalek means "iniquity and perversion." It is a type of the flesh. The Lord will have war with Amalek from generation to generation.

In many ways we are our own biggest enemy. It is not the devil. It is not your wife, your husband, your children, or the people you work with. None of these is your biggest enemy.

Your biggest enemy is YOU. No one can stop God from blessing you. No one can stop God from using you, except YOU. If this is true, then we must get out of the way and work with God instead of against Him. Prayer and fasting helps us to do this.

The Power of Humility and Prayer

While Moses was praying, Joshua was on the battlefield fighting. When Moses' hands were up, the soldiers were victorious in the battle. As soon as his hands came down, the soldiers began to lose the battle.

It was not a matter of how well equipped or how many there were in the army. It was a matter of whether there was prayer going up to God in heaven, and whether God's people were obedient to the revelation He gave them.

When God's people do what they are supposed to do, then the battle that goes on in heaven assures the positive outcome of the battles on earth. God says:

> *If my people who are called by My Name will humble themselves and pray and seek my face, and turn from their wicked ways, then I will hear from heaven, and will forgive their sin and heal their land. (2 Chronicles 7:14)*

He does not say, "If the politicians humble themselves and pray." He does not say, "If the generals or the admirals or the air force or the army or the navy humble themselves and pray." God places the responsibility for the healing of the land squarely on the shoulders of His people—the Christians.

Our hope is in God. We have to teach our children how to pray and to set their hope in God and in His Word. Everything else is unstable. God's Word is unchanging and brings stability into every area of our lives.

Give the Devil No Place

The Bible speaks so strongly against putting your spirit in communication with other spirits. God considers it an abomination for humans to link their spirits with demonic spirits to try to receive revelation. Sometimes, doing so can have long-lasting effects on a person's life.

I know one young girl who, when she was sixteen years of age was involved in a séance at the high school she attended. She called on spirits and an evil spirit entered into this young girl's life. From that time on she started writing weird, morbid poetry. She walked around clothed in depression, like death warmed up. And then a thought came into her mind that she was a re-incarnated poet.

She went to the local library to research this poet. She found out that there was actually a man by the name she was given that lived a few of hundred years beforehand. She pulled out his books and discovered that her poetry was remarkably similar to what this man wrote hundreds of years before.

The Bible talks about familiar spirits. They are demon spirits that are familiar with our lives and the events that surround our lives.

When a person goes to a fortune-teller and/or psychic to try to find out the future, they open the door to evil spirits. When people consult with any kind of spirit other than the Spirit of God about their future, they commit spiritual adultery because our spirits were designed by God to have communication with Him, and Him alone.

This young girl came to church to try and receive Christ as her Savior. As soon as she spoke the first syllable "Je…, she was knocked flat on the floor. After awhile she stood back up on her feet and tried once again to call on the Lord. She would say, "Je..." again and was knocked on the floor. She did this over and over. Every time, the same thing would happen.

Finally, at about one o'clock a.m., we successfully cast the devil out of this girl. She received Christ as her Lord and Savior, went to Bible College and became full of the Word and the Holy Spirit. The joy of the Lord became her strength and there was no more depression or weird, morbid poetry. The Bible tells us there are different kinds of demon spirits, and some will come out only by prayer and fasting.

The Anointing Destroys Yokes

Some demons leave as soon as a Spirit-filled Christian comes into the room. Other people who are oppressed by demons come into church and are set free when anointed praise and worship begins.

When King Saul was tormented with evil spirits, David would play anointed music, and as a result, the tormenting demons departed from King Saul (1 Samuel 16:13).

Others are set free when they hear the Word preached. There are others set free when the spirits are cast out in Jesus' Name.

However, there are others where demon powers have established a stronghold in their lives. They may have been in their family for generations and no one has broken their power, so they are passed on to the next generation.

Some people have a nasty, sarcastic disposition. Many times this is not the person's natural personality, but a principality that has gained entrance perhaps through that person dabbling in witchcraft, tarot cards, Ouija boards, or seeking fortunetellers.

If you have been involved in the occult, ask God to forgive you, and renounce these things because they can cause depression, disease, divorce and disaster in your life.

Renounce the Works of Darkness

We fast to loose the bands of wickedness, to cast out strong demonic powers, and to rid ourselves of doubt and unbelief so we can pass on a generational blessing to our children instead of a generational curse.

If you have been involved in the occult, and you pray this prayer and mean it, you can be free.

> Father, in the Name of Jesus, I come to you. And I ask that you forgive me for my sins, for any involvement in the occult, in Ouija boards,

tarot cards, fortunetellers, and any other kind of black magic, white magic, or divination. I renounce these things and declare that they will not be a part of my life any more. Go from me, in Jesus Name.

And Father, thank you for the blood of Jesus that cleanses me and washes me from all sin. Thank you Lord Jesus. Fill me with Your Holy Spirit. Help me to be sensitive to the Spirit of God. The Bible says that they that worship the Father must worship Him in spirit and in truth. So Father, I thank you that I can worship you with my spirit. I put my spirit in communication with your Spirit that I might hear your voice, understand your plan, have revival and restoration in my life, my family, my local church, and across this nation, in Jesus' mighty Name. Thank You, Lord Jesus.

Pray Without Ceasing

Hazel and I believe there is going to be major breakthrough in the Middle East. God loves the Middle Easterners and is not willing that any of them perish, but come to the knowledge of salvation through Jesus Christ (2 Peter 3:9).

The Arab people are not the problem. Radical Islam is the problem. A lot of people in the Middle East are searching after God.

When we pray for the peace of Jerusalem, we are praying for the blinders to be taken off the eyes of the Jews so they can be saved.

There will be no peace until the Prince of Peace comes into people's hearts. When we pray for peace in the Middle East, we are really praying for mass conversion of people into Christianity. That is what we are praying for.

Nobody wants to emigrate to Iraq, Iran, Afghanistan, India, China, and Russia—places where religions such as Islam, Communism, Hinduism, and Buddhism have established a major stronghold. What have these religions ever done for their nations? Nothing, except they have kept the people in bondage.

People want to immigrate to countries where Christianity has been the major influence for generations. They want to immigrate to the United States, Canada, England, Australia, New Zealand and Western Europe. They want to immigrate to the nations where the gospel has gone forth in the past, and established the main foundational beliefs, practices and culture of the area. What has Christianity done for the nations that used to be called Christendom? EVERYTHING.

It is all because of the goodness and grace of God. "*Every good and every perfect gift is from above, and comes down from the Father of lights, with whom there is no variation or shadow of turning*" (James 1:17). Whatever we bind on earth is bound in heaven. Whatever we loose on earth is loosed in heaven (Matthew 16:19). My prayer is, "*Father, let Your kingdom come and Your will be done on earth as it is heaven*" (Matthew 6:10)!!!

8

Three Dimensions of Time

The Scriptures speak of three dimensions of time: God's working time, Satan's fighting time and our standing time, and they all happen at the same time. There is personal warfare, where Satan's strategy is to either take us out of the battle, or get us fighting against our own soldiers.

The apostle Paul tells us to, *"put on the whole armor of God, that we may be able to withstand in the evil day, and having done all to stand. Stand therefore"* (Ephesians 6:13-14). We all have evil days, times when we receive bad news: a negative report from a doctor that you or someone close to you has a life threatening disease; a report from the accountant of impending financial disaster; a bad report of family problems, accidents, or a potential church split. How we respond during these crucial times makes the difference between continued success and victory or failure and defeat. How do we stand, and what is happening in the spirit realm while we stand?

Satan's Fighting Time

In the parable, "The Sower Sows the Word" (Mark 4:13-20), the Scripture declares that after the Word had been sown in the hearts of people, "*Satan comes immediately* to steal *the Word* that was sown in the heart (4:15). Also, when persecution and affliction arises for the Word's sake, many are offended (4:17). Offences will come, but dealing with them is part of growing up spiritually. Satan will fight you for every piece of revelation you receive from the Word of God to stop you from being useful and fruitful in the kingdom. If you let him, he will try to do it immediately before the truth has time to take root.

God's Working Time

> *The king's heart is in the hand of the Lord, like the rivers of water; He turns it wherever He wishes (Proverbs 21:1).*

God will not overrule a person's will, but He does have ways of changing a person's will. He can make the circumstances around a person's life become so miserable that they are willing to change. Jonah is a good example of this. During our standing time God is working and making preparations in three areas.

Working in your life

God develops your character so that you can be trusted more fully. He prepares and positions you to fulfill His purposes. He brings healing to your past so that it does not pollute or sabotage your future.

Working in your circumstances

God knows how to make the circumstances work for you or against you. Romans 8:28 implies that if you love God and are seeking after His purposes you will find no favor outside of the purpose of God for your life. I used to panic when my plans seemed to be failing, but now I have come to realize that many times things go wrong to make me more right. Some of the things I struggle with actually help push me into the will of God.

Working in the lives of others

"God stirred the heart of King Cyrus" (Ezra 1:1). God knows how to stir and change the hearts of mankind, but it usually takes time. When my wife began to pray and fast for my salvation the Lord began to move upon my heart and soften it towards the gospel. The Lord put all kinds of people in my path; in fact it seemed like everywhere I went I would be confronted with the gospel message in one way or another.

Our Standing Time

> *For we do not wrestle against flesh and blood, but against principalities, against powers, against the rulers of the darkness of this age, against spiritual hosts of wickedness in the heavenly places. Therefore take up the whole armor of God, that you may be able to withstand in* ***the evil day*** *and having done all, to* ***stand. Stand therefore.*** *(Ephesians 6:12-14)*

When the evil day comes we must know how to stand and overcome.

What does it mean to stand? How long should we stand? Psalm 112:7 says, *"He will not be afraid of evil tidings; his heart is fixed trusting in the Lord."* Many people do not have faith when they really need it—when they get evil tidings. However, it is amazing how things can change if we keep standing. To stand means *to hold your ground and keep pushing forward.* It involves faith and trust.

We need trust when we do not understand what is happening and our experience does not match up with what the Word says. When what is happening to us does not seem right, this is the time that we have to know God well enough to be able to say, "Lord, I don't understand, it doesn't seem right, *nevertheless,* **I trust You**."

During our standing time we must be careful to keep our hearts and attitudes right. During times like these, we can become better, or bitter. During times of trial we must run to God, not away from Him, and we must trust Him to bring us through victorious. The more we trust Him the more we will trust in His plan. We are not promised instant victory, but we are promised the victory if we continue to stand in faith, hope, trust and integrity.

Power of a Fasted Life

Look at the opposition that came against the apostle Paul. In Acts 13, they prayed, fasted and received direction from God. They were sent forth by the Holy Ghost into Holy Spirit directed and empowered service. They went to Cyprus and then to Paphos, where a sorcerer withstood them to their face, seeking to turn the proconsul away from the faith. Paul experienced satanic opposition right off the bat.

Then Paul, full of the Holy Ghost, stood up and said, "*O full of all deceit and fraud, you son of the devil, you enemy of righteousness, will you not cease perverting the straight ways of the Lord*?" He called down the judgment of God and the sorcerer was struck blind. The Scripture goes on to say, "*Then the proconsul believed*"(Acts 13:12). When faced with opposition, Paul knew how to stand and keep pushing forward in faith until the breakthrough came.

Another time, Paul had a vision of a man from Macedonia standing and pleading with him saying, "*Come over to Macedonia and help us*" (Acts 16: 9).

Paul immediately jumped on a boat and took the gospel to Europe and planted Europe's first ever church in a place in Greece called Philippi. When he arrived in Philippi, he went down to the riverside on the Sabbath day where prayer was customarily made and sat down and spoke to a group of women. God opened the heart of a certain woman, named Lydia, to the things Paul spoke. She and her household were baptized and she opened her house to Paul and his company (Acts 16:11-15).

Right after that Paul encountered a little psychic woman telling fortunes. She had a spirit of divination.

> *These men are the servants of the Most High God, who proclaim to us the way of salvation.* (Acts 16:17)

What she said was right, but it was an evil spirit speaking through her. She followed Paul for many days. Finally Paul, being greatly annoyed, turned and said to the spirit, "*I command you in the name of Jesus Christ to come out of her. And he came out that very hour*" (Acts 16:18). The woman was totally set free. She could no longer tell fortunes and thus lost her psychic business.

The two men that were prostituting her became so angry they had Paul and Silas thrown in jail. Instead of saying, "Oh God, this isn't fair," Paul and Silas began to worship and praise God (Acts 16:19-25).

They had so much faith in God that they would not allow anything to take the Word out of their mouths. Nothing was going to take the song of praise and victory out of their hearts. They praised so loud and with so much gusto that all the prisoners heard them.

While they were praising and worshiping, God sent an earthquake. The foundations of the prison were shaken. All the doors of the prison were opened. Everyone's chains were loosed. The jailer and his whole house were saved and baptized, and the church at Philippi was planted (Acts 16:26-32).

My wife and I could tell you all kinds of stories about demonic opposition and breakthroughs we have seen. We have been in revival and know what revival is like.

In revival, you can preach on almost any subject, it seems, and people run down the aisles weeping, repenting, and wanting to receive Christ.

Things are different in revival because God's Spirit moves

in a unique way. So often, it demands corporate obedience. Corporate obedience brings corporate blessing. One disobedient person can stop the blessing for a whole group (See Numbers 12:14-15).

It is time to seek God with all of our hearts, to hear His voice, and then do what He tells us so we can get the breakthroughs that we need and take the gospel message around the world. And, we must not forget that God is continually working in our behalf to cause *all things to work together for good* because we love God and are the called according to His purpose (Romans 8:28).

9

Overcoming Faith

Can You Believe?

In Mark's gospel, chapter 9, there was a young man having convulsions or epileptic fits and it was discerned that the force behind the convulsions was an evil spirit.

> *Then one of the crowd answered and said, "Teacher, I brought You my son, who has a mute spirit. And wherever it seizes him, it throws him down; he foams at the mouth, gnashes his teeth, and becomes rigid. So I spoke to Your disciples, that they should cast it out, but they could not." He answered him and said, "O faithless generation, how long shall I be with you? How long shall I bear with you? Bring him to Me." (Mark 9:17-19)*

Jesus was saying, "I have given you all the power and authority you need. So what is your problem?" He called them a *faithless generation*!

By now the disciples should have been operating in faith and power, but they were not, so Jesus said, *"How long am I going to be with you? Bring him to Me."* He was saying, "Look, I am not going to be with you forever. You are going to have to increase your faith to be able to do these things after I am gone."

> *Then they brought him to Him. And when he saw Him, immediately the spirit convulsed him, and he fell on the ground and wallowed, foaming at the mouth. So He asked his father, "How long has this been happening to him?" And he said, "From childhood. And often he has thrown him both into the fire and into the water to destroy him. But if You can do anything, have compassion on us and help us."*

Jesus said to him, "*If you can believe, all things are possible to him who believes*" (Mark 9:20-23).

Jesus straightened out this man's theology. He essentially said, "It is not if I can do anything. It is **if you can believe**! ALL THINGS ARE POSSIBLE TO HIM THAT BELIEVES!"

> *Immediately the father of the child cried out and said with tears, "Lord, I believe; help my unbelief!" (Mark 9-24)*

Have you ever felt like that? In your heart you believe, but there are all these opposing forces assaulting your mind. Every time you look at the circumstances confusion sets in and your flesh begins to react. You wonder how deliverance and freedom can come. You cry out, "Lord, I believe. Help my unbelief."

When you cry out like that, thank God for responding with His mercy and grace.

> *When Jesus saw that the people came running together, He rebuked the unclean spirit, saying to it, "Deaf and dumb spirit, I command you, come out of him and enter him no more!"*

> *Then the spirit cried out, convulsed him greatly, and came out of him. And he became as one dead, so that many said, "He is dead."*
>
> *But Jesus took him by the hand and lifted him up, and he arose.*
>
> *And when He had come into the house, His disciples asked Him privately, "Why could we not cast it out?" (Mark 9:25-28)*

His disciples wanted to know why they could not cast out the deaf and dumb spirit. Some today might simply dismiss the matter and say, "Well, I guess it's not God's will."

But the disciples knew they should have been able to cast out demons and they wanted to know why they could not cast out this demon.

> *So He said to them, "This kind can come out by nothing but prayer and fasting." (Mark 9:29)*

In Matthew's account, it says:

> *So Jesus said to them, "**Because of your unbelief**... for assuredly, I say to you, if you have faith as a mustard seed, you will say to this mountain, 'Move from here to there,' and it will move; and nothing will be impossible for you." (Matthew 17:20)*

Jesus told the disciples the reason they could not cast out the evil spirit was because of their unbelief. In this instance, if they had fasted and prayed, they would have been able to cast the spirit out.

Why? Because when you fast and pray you become more sensitive to the things of God. Your discernment increases. You get more revelation on the Word of God. You become stronger in faith on the inside and you feel like you could do anything God tells you to do.

Another time, Jesus went to his hometown and He could do no mighty works there because of the people's unbelief, except He laid hands on a few sickly people and healed them (Mark 6:5).

Prayer, fasting and the teaching of God's Word is the cure for unbelief. "*Then He went about the villages in a circuit, teaching*" (Mark 6:6) because, "*faith comes by hearing and hearing by the Word of God*" (Romans 10:17). When the Word of God is believed and received, faith comes and unbelief goes.

The Word of God says that He has given believers authority in His Name.

> *And these signs will follow those who believe: In My name they will cast out demons; they will speak with new tongues; they will take up serpents; and if they drink anything deadly, it will by no means hurt them; they will lay hands on the sick, and they will recover. (Mark 16:17-18)*

We have the authority, but do we believe? Time and time again the gospels record Jesus saying, "*according to your faith, be it unto you.*" We can either believe and receive, or doubt and go without!

10

Repentance, Revival and Restoration

The ultimate purpose of fasting is for restoration, revival and the salvation of souls. All the other reasons for fasting are to help make this happen.

> *For thus says the High and Lofty One Who inhabits eternity, Whose Name is Holy: "I dwell in the high and holy place, with him who has a contrite and humble spirit, to revive the spirit of the humble, and to revive the heart of the contrite ones." (Isaiah 57:15)*

God dwells in the Most High Place with those who are humble and repentant. When you dwell with God and God dwells with you, then something happens in you. Your heart and spirit become revived, and that which was dead comes back to life. The desire and hunger for the Word of God and the things of God come back. Your love for the church is restored and you cannot wait to get to church.

A revived heart is enthusiastic and passionate. A revived heart is responsive to the promptings of the Holy Spirit and quick to obey His commands.

The Pattern of Revival

> *If My people who are called by My name will humble themselves, and pray and seek My face, and turn from their wicked ways, then I will hear from heaven, and will forgive their sin and heal their land. (2 Chronicles 7:14)*

There are six things we can see from this passage:

1. God's People Begin to Cry Out in Prayer

This happens when you get sick and tired of being sick and tired. When you get fed up being sick, sad and sinful, and from all of the consequences that result from it, then you begin to cry out to God. Desperation leads people to this kind of prayer.

2. God Comes on the Scene

After you cry out in prayer, God begins to show up in new ways because you have been calling on Him. You draw near to Him and He draws near to you.

3. The People Repent

When God shows up, people repent. When God comes on the scene, we are convicted of even small acts of disobedience and we truly repent. It is impossible to come into the presence of a God, who is described in Isaiah 6:3 as *"Holy, holy, holy,"* without feeling your need for repentance and cleansing.

4. God Revives the People

God revives the repentant ones. He says, *" I dwell in the high and holy place, with him who has a contrite and humble spirit, to revive the spirit of the humble, and to revive the heart of the contrite ones"* (Isaiah 57:15). When God comes on the scene, a revival begins to take place within you.

5. The People Begin to Minister and Pour Out Their Lives Into Others

Once you become revived on the inside, you begin to think about the salvation of others. You say within yourself, "I can't keep this to myself. My mother needs it. My dad needs it. My sister needs it. The people I work with need it. My next-door neighbor needs it. And somehow, some way I am going to reach them. I cannot and must not keep it to myself."

Like the Apostle Paul said, "*I am a debtor*" (Romans 1:14). I owe it to them. I have something they do not. I have love, joy, peace, and victory. Everybody needs what I have; freely I have received, and freely I will give (Matthew 10:8).

Then you begin to pour yourself out for others, realizing your life is not just about you. God has blessed us to be a blessing to others.

6. God Empowers for Service

There is an anointing to change *you*, and then there is an anointing that empowers you to help others. "*The Spirit of the Lord is upon me and He has anointed me*" (Luke 4:18). For what purpose does He anoint?

> *...To preach the gospel to the poor; He has sent Me to heal the brokenhearted, to proclaim liberty to the captives and recovery of sight to the blind, to set at liberty those who are oppressed; to proclaim the acceptable year of the Lord. (Luke 4:18-19)*

The anointing is to preach the gospel, heal and set people free. God equips and empowers us and gives us ability above and beyond our own ability. By faith, we use what we have, and then He makes up the difference.

Mark 16:20 says: "*And they [the disciples] went out and preached everywhere, the Lord working with them and confirming the word through the accompanying signs.*" As you begin to move out in faith you will experience God's anointing, and this Scripture will start to become a reality in your life. Then you will begin living a supernatural lifestyle.

I don't know about you, but I don't want a superficial life. I want *a supernatural life*. You can have superficial Christianity or you can have a supernatural walk with God. It is up to you. God wants to revive us so he can use us.

> *Repent therefore and be converted, that your sins may be blotted out, so that times of refreshing may come from the presence of the Lord, and that He may send Jesus Christ, who was preached to you before, whom heaven must receive until the times of restoration of all things, which God has spoken by the mouth of all His holy prophets since the world began. (Acts 3:19-21)*

Notice the pattern once again. We cry out to God, He comes on the scene. We get convicted, repent, and then times of refreshing come from the presence of the Lord. With the refreshing comes revelation concerning our future. We begin to see what we have never seen before and hear what we have never heard before. This enables us to be able to do what we have never done before.

Last Days: Restoration

In the last days there will be a restoration of all things spoken by the prophets. God says

> *In the last days I will pour out My Spirit on all flesh, your sons and your daughters shall prophesy, your old men shall dream dreams, your young men shall see visions. And also on My menservants and on My maidservants I will pour out My Spirit in those days. (Joel 2:28-29)*

> *Verily, verily, I say unto you, He that believeth on*

> *Me, the works that I do shall he do also; and greater [works] than these shall he do, because I go unto My Father. (John 14:12)*

There will be a restoration of everything that was prophesied and promised to the church. There will be a return back to New Testament Christianity, glory to God, where we have a church full of prayer, a church full of power, a church full of praise, a church full of people, and a church full of divine happenings all of the time—that is what I call normal New Testament Christianity.

You only need to revive something when it has died. You must revive it to bring it back to normal. It is like a car battery when it is flat. All the parts are there; there just is no charge in it. So you put a reverse charge through it to bring it back to its full power so it will start your car, power the lights, the CD player and whatever else you have in your car. The electrical accessories will do what they are supposed to do when the car battery is fully charged. God is about to super-charge His Church and bring all who are within it back to full power.

It begins with repentance, and afterward times of refreshing will come from God. Then divine revelation and renewal, and out of that whole thing comes restoration. Everything the devil has taken away from us God begins to restore back to us.

> Lord, we will give you no rest, until we see Your Church restored back to full power and established as a praise upon the earth! (Isaiah 62:7)

Different Kinds of Revivals

There are many different kinds of revivals. There are revivals that affect the conscience; revivals that affect the mind; revivals of restoration of a biblical experience; and revivals where there has been an area of neglect.

Revivals that Affect the Conscience

The revival of Charles Finney's day in the 19th century was one that affected the conscience. Prayer warriors went into the city before Finney arrived to prepare the way. When Finney did arrive, just his presence would cause many people to break down and begin to repent.

A few years back, there was a revival like this in Pensacola, Florida. The consciences of people were pricked by the Word and the Spirit, and multiplied thousands repented.

In the latter part of the twentieth century, there was a revival in North America that affected the emotions; joy and the ability to laugh were restored to hundreds of thousands of people who had been oppressed and depressed. People with no peace entered into the peace of God that surpasses all understanding. This was a revival that affected the emotions.

Revivals that Affect the Mind

Revivals that affect the mind usher in a new way of thinking. The Word of Faith movement was the restoration of a biblical truth.

Kenneth Hagin, Sr. had a revelation concerning the God kind of faith.

> *Whosoever shall say unto this mountain, Be thou removed, and be thou cast into the sea; and shall not doubt in his heart, but shall believe that those things which he saith shall come to pass; he shall have whatsoever he saith. Therefore I say to you, whatsoever things you desire when you pray believe that you receive them and you shall have them. (Mark 11:22-24, KJV)*

This revelation came forth in the mid 1970s; it was a revelation that captured the imaginations of people as they began to realize it was possible for the ordinary believer to grow stronger in faith and to believe for the miraculous. They began to speak faith, pray in faith, and to live by a new dimension of faith. This was called the Word Movement; people studied, memorized, meditated, and sang the Word of God. Conferences had hardly any music at all. The speakers would come in, open their Bibles and teach from nine o'clock in the morning until eleven o'clock at night. Then the people would leave with all kinds of tapes and books hungering after deeper insights into God's Word. This brought a new way of thinking and a new way of living to the church.

Martin Luther, who started the Reformation movement in the Sixteenth Century, restored a fundamental truth to the church that had been lost during the Dark Ages, that is, "*the just shall live by faith*" (Hebrews 10:38). We do not have to do penance or any of the other things we were told we have to do to be saved. We are "*saved by grace through faith [in the Lord Jesus Christ] and not by works lest any man should boast*" (Ephesians 2:8-9). This was the mighty revelation that brought forth the Protestant Reformation.

Revivals through Restoration of Biblical Experiences

There are whole revivals that came through the restoration of a biblical experience that had been lost. For instance, the Baptists restored water baptism and people began to be baptized in water following conversion. The Pentecostals restored the baptism of the Holy Spirit at the beginning of the last century. People experienced the baptism of the Holy Spirit and began to speak in other tongues, a biblical experience that was neglected for centuries.

Then there was the Charismatic Revival. That was a revival around the gifts of the Holy Ghost. People began to realize that God has given these gifts to the church: the gifts of healings, the working of miracles, the gift of faith, the gift of tongues and the gift of interpretation, the gift of prophecy, word of knowledge, word of wisdom, discerning of spirits, and he has divided severally to every man as He wills (1 Corinthians 12:7-11). People began to get hold of these truths and there was a restoration of biblical spiritual experiences that had been lost for years.

Revivals through an Area of Neglect Being Fulfilled

There are revivals where there is an area of neglect. This is very often where Para-church ministries have sprung up to fill a void or an area that the local church had neglected.

For example, lay people were not being used to any great degree in the local church. As a result, few leaders were being raised up. Full Gospel Businessmen and Women's Aglow came on the scene and began to involve lay people in ministry. Then it seemed like almost overnight spiritual leaders were coming out of the woodwork. Many of those who came out of Full Gospel Businessmen and Women's Aglow eventually ended up as great pastors, evangelists, key workers in the church, and effective ministers all around the world.

YWAM came on the scene because world missions were being neglected. Local churches gave little opportunity for their people to be involved in missions. So YWAM sprung up and there was a revival through people being trained and released to go on the mission field.

In the 1990's, organizations like Promise Keepers and Focus on the Family came on the scene. Promise Keepers ministered to men, and Focus on the Family came to minister to families.

The reason Para-church ministries are raised up by the Lord is because the local church is not doing what it is supposed to do. These ministries really show us where there is a major area of neglect in the Body of Christ at a given time.

Revivals come to meet the needs. Philippians 4:19 says, "*My God shall supply all of our needs according to His riches in glory by*

Christ Jesus." Very often a thriving Para-church ministry reveals a lack in the local church.

When the church sees an organization like Promise Keepers ministering to and mobilizing men, then it should realize that there needs to be ministry to and mobilization of men in the local church.

There are different kinds of revivals in different nations at different times. Whatever the area of need is, God begins to move, revive, restore, replenish, and meet the needs.

What is the need where you are? What is the need in the United States? What areas of lack are there in the local church? What is the lack in your personal life? What do you personally need? Even though the needs are different, they are basically the same. Whether you are from China, India, Africa, Europe, South America, the United States, or any other nation of the world, there are certain basic needs that are the same.

There are also needs that are specific to the region. God understands what they are and, by His grace, will make a way for the needs to be met.

Southern California's Need

Before my wife and I moved to California in 2001 we said, "Lord, we do not want to simply duplicate what other ministers and churches are already doing in California. We need to see the area of need; show us the vacuum and how we can fill it." We came to California and spied out the land and saw many great churches and ministers that were doing great things for God. But the one area of need we did see that did not seem to be fully met was the raising up and releasing of leaders into Holy Spirit directed service. This is an area in which Hazel and I have had major experience and great success during our prior twenty-six years of ministry. The Apostolic Vision of Victory Churches International creates so many opportunities; we are always in need of new leaders to take advantage of these opportunities. The God-given ability on our lives has enabled us to attract, raise up and release multiplied thousands of leaders into full-time Christian service.

When my wife and I came to California God said," Don't take any Canadians with you." Many of our staff and leaders wanted to come with us, but the Lord had spoken clearly to our hearts that to take Canadians with us would be like taking Uriah's little ewe lamb (2 Samuel 12:1-4). In other words, Canada needs every leader it has. In obedience to the Lord we came alone to California. However, in California there are so many Christians who are trained, full of the Word and have a lot of experience and need to be released into Holy Spirit directed service. The Lord promised to bring leaders to us and He has been faithful to do it.

We started California Victory Church in 2001. Three months after we started, a vibrant church in the area close to where we were located went through major problems that left many people broken, hurting and disillusioned. In January 2002 three hundred of these same people walked through the doors of our new church, many of them leaders. Through prayer, fasting and seeking God, Hazel and I ended up in the right place, at the right time, with the right anointing to be able to bring healing, hope and eventually release to many of these gifted leaders. How profitable it is to the Kingdom of God when you are where God wants you to be, doing what God wants you to do, with what He has given you. The grace and mercy of God never ceases to amaze us.

What we see as one of the biggest needs in North America is the release of ministry; for every born again believer to start to minister in whatever gift God has given them to help build up the Body of Christ and become everything God has called them to be.

In Southern California, in a fifty-mile radius from where we live, so many great moves of God have started. That shows you that there is something special about this area. It shows you this is good soil. It shows you something that is very positive about the people here.

So we look at what the real needs are, because we know our God wants to meet the real needs of the people; and when we work together with God to help meet the needs, we enter into the realm of the supernatural (Philippians 4:19).

Elements for Revival

I see three elements needed for revival to take place:

1. The Sovereignty of God
2. The conditions in the world and the church
3. The preparedness of man and the church

The Sovereignty of God

Any revival is always the Sovereign move of God. Every time you see a revival, God is moving in His Sovereignty. Nevertheless, He moves at specific times. These times are when you have a backslidden, apathetic, complacent, lukewarm church, or when the world is in such a desperate condition that God has to intervene.

The Conditions in the World and the Church

God's divine intervention is desperately needed in the world today, but whenever God is going to do something wonderful, He starts with a difficulty. Whenever He is going to do something *very* wonderful, He starts with a seeming impossibility.

Only God can save our families. Only God can save our churches.

We need God's presence, power, protection, and provision! We need His wisdom, guidance, and direction!

That means we have to stay close to Him. Prayer and fasting can bring divine intervention into a world that is in a mess, and a church that needs reviving and restoring.

In Judges 6, Israel was in complete bondage to a cruel

enemy—conditions could hardly be worse. Yet, when the people began to cry out to God, He heard them and sent a deliverer. A man called Gideon defeated an army of over one hundred twenty thousand soldiers with an army of three hundred trained, unified, anointed men, each one standing in his place and doing his part. God can still do more with less.

The Preparedness of Man and the Church

This does not mean the whole church is prepared, but some are. Everybody in Israel's army in Gideon's day was not prepared, but three hundred were. On the Day of Pentecost, everybody in Jerusalem wasn't prepared, but one hundred and twenty were. God always has a prepared people that he can use in every generation.

At the turn of the 20th Century, there were a handful of people in a little building on Azusa Street in Los Angeles who had been crying out to God for spiritual rain. The Holy Spirit was poured out on them and they began speaking in other tongues. From this event, the experience of Pentecost (Acts 2) was restored. People from around the world began to cry out to God and be filled with the Holy Spirit and speak in other tongues. This was the beginning of the modern day Pentecostal movement which gave birth to a multitude of new, Full-Gospel, Pentecostal, Apostolic, first generational pioneer movements, that eventually became major denominations. Over the last century this movement exploded around the world with the planting of hundreds of thousands of fresh, new vibrant churches.

Church Planting Revivals

North America needs more first-generational pioneer movements. There is something exciting about being part of a first-generational pioneer movement that you do not experience anywhere else.

The biggest revivals that have ever taken place were church planting movements. The Methodists were a church planting movement with John Wesley. He had a systematic plan on how to plant churches all around the world. Then the Pentecostal Assemblies came along at a later date. They didn't have a plan, but it just happened spontaneously by the Holy Ghost.

I believe the last great move of God will encompass both the Methodist and the Pentecostal movements. It will be a move that has an aggressive, strategic plan to plant churches all around the world, together with a spontaneous move of the Holy Ghost.

The greatest moves of God have always been church planting movements. You can do more with a thousand churches across a nation than you can with one, no matter how large that one may be. A country needs one good church for every two thousand people to be effectively evangelized. Every real move of God's Spirit will result in the saving of souls, the raising up of leaders and the planting of fresh, new, vibrant churches.

Intercessors, we need you to stand in the gap and pray for whatever kind of revival is needed in your area. It is time for the militant, miraculous, and triumphant church to arise and be about our Father's business!!!

11

Victory, a First-Generational Pioneer Movement

Spirit of the Pioneer

Every generation needs a first generational pioneer movement. Settlers never want to go any further, but pioneers are always going beyond the present boundaries.

Settlers are more the managers and maintainers of what the pioneers have started. Both are essential to the long-term development and expansion of God's kingdom. The Lord will not give us more than we are able to maintain.

Pioneers are visionaries and are willing to put up with what is less than ideal, because of what they see happening in the future. They are willing to sacrifice something small today for something gigantic tomorrow.

"In the beginning God created..." (Genesis 1:1) Our God is the Creator and we are created in His image. That means there is a creative side to us all that needs to be made manifest. A creator can make something out of nothing. Entrepreneurs have

a pioneer spirit and are able to create something visible out of that which is invisible. When we draw close to God and talk to Him in prayer, and spend time in His presence, He floods our hearts and minds with His ways and ideas. Every good income-producing idea you have ever had came from God. Just one of God's ideas can move the church ahead by leaps and bounds.

Some people are praying for a move of God. We need to pray for a move of the church! God is already moving. When the church gets in synch with the Lord, the people that God has called as pioneers will begin to rise up with fresh creative ways of reaching people, new ways of generating finances, buying buildings, creating great anointed gospel music, and new ways of taking the gospel to the world.

Sixty thousand churches came out of the Welsh Revival at the beginning of the twentieth century. This revival spread into a movement that went into more than sixty nations of the world. One of those nations was Canada. Several years ago they asked me to be the main speaker for their national conference.

They said, "We want you to give us a prod back to our roots." They had heard we were apostolic. We were the fastest growing group of churches in Canada at that particular time. We had thirty percent growth every year for twelve years. You would do pretty well if you had a business doing that.

They asked, "Where did you learn about being apostolic? Where did you hear about the apostolic?"

I told them I read about the five-fold ministry in the Bible. I had also read some of their denomination's books and knew that they had written about the five-fold ministry many, many years ago. They said, "Where did you learn to work together in an apostolic team ministry?"

I said, "Well, I didn't. We just did it and then we figured out afterwards what it was." We did not figure out what it was first and then try to do it. We simply did it and wrote it up really quickly before we forgot what we did. That is how we got our policies and procedures for Victory Churches International. And if it does not work, then we will change it, because we are not going to be bound by rules and regulations or policies and procedures. They are only there to keep us on track.

Apostolic History

The Victory Church movement has an apostolic history of planting churches, raising up ministers, and releasing people—not just into church planting, but also into television, politics, music, education, business, and into every realm of society.

Apostolic Leadership

We have apostolic leadership—that means apostles, prophets, evangelists, pastors and teachers working together in our organization, for the equipping of the saints for the work of the ministry (Ephesians 4:11-12).

Apostolic Doctrine

We have apostolic doctrine, which means we believe in the gifts and power of the Holy Ghost. We believe in being filled with the Holy Ghost and speaking in tongues.

Apostolic Vision

We have an apostolic vision, which is a worldwide vision—a vision that is bigger than any one of us, a vision that is bigger than your family, church, city or nation. It is a worldwide vision.

Apostolic Future

Apostolic describes how the church began on the day of Pentecost, how it continued throughout the book of Acts, and how it is going to close out the church age. It will be a glorious, victorious, miraculous church with Christ-like believers and churches in even the most remote corners of the earth.

The battle is not over your past or your present—it is over your future, and your future is not just about you, but is inclusive of all those that God wants to bless through you. The future is worth fighting for. We must know what we are fighting for, love what we are fighting for, and fight with passion for the souls of those who do not yet know Jesus. The future belongs to those who are willing to invest in it—and for those who do, the best is yet to come!

Hazel and I moved to Orange County, California in 2001, and when we first looked around we thought this must be one of the most difficult places in the world to plant a church, because the people have seen everything, heard everything, done everything, and have everything. The Lord spoke to my heart and said, "If you can break through here, you can change the world from this place."

There are so many talented, gifted individuals around here. There is dynamic spiritual energy here that is infectious. You can feel it. There is something here that many Californians may take for granted. What you find here is not found everywhere in the world, I can assure you.

So many great ministries started from this place because of the good soil. We have found so many of the people in Southern California to be positive, generous, big-thinking risk-takers, and it certainly takes these kinds of qualities to be able to do anything substantial for the Kingdom of God.

The Key to Timing is Preparation

God has people throughout the whole world who are already prepared and positioned. They are just waiting for the Holy Ghost to separate them for the work they are called by God to do. Those who have become too comfortable and have lost the pioneer spirit can be changed through prayer and fasting. Let us pray that no one will be able to sit on the back seat doing nothing while they are so full of gifts, talent, abilities, and creativity. God is stirring up the gifts He has placed within us and is thrusting us all back onto the front lines to win souls and build His Church.

We have to make sure we are prepared. It means taking every step of faith that God calls us to take. If you have never been water baptized, you need to be, as a step of faith and obedience unto God, which helps to take you to another level.

The Bible says that the promise of being filled with the Holy Spirit is for you, your children, and your children's children, and to all who are far off (Acts 2:38-39). If you have never been filled with the Holy Ghost with the evidence of speaking in other tongues, then you need to decide in your heart that you are going to receive that baptism. Know without a shadow of doubt that it is for you, and you can receive it today!

With this kind of attitude you can be filled with the Holy Spirit right now! In Acts 10, while Peter was speaking, the Holy Ghost fell on all those that heard the Word and they began to speak with other tongues (10:44-45).

Life is lived on levels. It is arrived at by stages. After you are born again, water baptism takes you to a new level. Baptism in the Holy Ghost takes you to a greater level. Pioneers always want to go further. Pioneers are willing to go where they have never been before and do what they have never done before in order to obey God.

Keep that pioneer spirit stirred up through prayer and fasting, and together, we will be World Shakers and History Makers!!!

12

Revive Us O' Lord

Revive me according to Your word. (Psalm 119:25)

We need a revival that so pricks the conscience that people not only repent but also make restitution where possible. We cannot always make everything right that we have done wrong, but some things we can. Among the things that Christians will be convicted of is the withholding of tithes and offerings. I believe that many will bring their back tithes to the house of the Lord and make it right.

In the Old Testament they had to add twenty percent to the tithe if they withheld it. If you have never tithed, this is the time to make the decision and begin to tithe. The Lord says, " *Try me now in this, if I will not open for you the windows of heaven and pour out for you such blessing that there will not be room enough to receive it*" (Malachi 3:10).

I am talking about revival. If you are revived, then you are going to obey His Word. When you obey, then you keep moving on and the power of God keeps flowing through you. As soon as you disobey, everything stops.

When we fast, old habits are broken off of us and we receive fresh revelation from God. Then we have an opportunity to establish the right kind of habits and attitudes that will bring life, blessing, and fresh vision.

General DeGaulle said, "If you do big things, you attract big people. If you do little things, you attract little people. And little people cause you problems."

It is very difficult to put a big vision into a little mind. Little minds are easily threatened. We have to begin to see it big and keep it simple. So many people see it small and then they complicate it.

We want to do it big, do it good, and do it together.

Dwight Moody said, "If God is your partner, then make your plans big." We serve a big God!

It is time for giant killers and the big thinking, risk-takers to arise. I believe the Lord wants to use His church to bless the world in bigger and greater ways than ever before.

When we look at the condition of the world today it is easy to see that the world needs revival. When we look at the church today we can see that it is being pruned, prepared, and positioned for the greatest revival this world has ever seen. The key to timing is preparation and it can take years of preparation for what may appear to be overnight success.

One of the last moves of God was the refreshing movement. During this move we did not take any new territory, we just got back some of the things the devil had stolen.

Now enough people in the church have gotten their strength, their joy and their victory back and are saying, "Here I am Lord, use me".

Nevertheless, we must remember that true revival is a sovereign move of God.

Revival is like surfing. The surfer does not make the wave. The surfer just has to be ready to ride the wave.

God is the one who makes the wave. But we have to prepare so that we are ready and properly positioned when it does come.

Can you see it with the eyes of faith? Can you hear what the Spirit is saying to the church today? "*Sanctify yourselves for tomorrow the Lord will do wonders among you*" (Joshua 3:5). Get ready for tomorrow's move today! Do it now!

Declare with me:

> Father of Glory, give unto me the Spirit of wisdom and revelation in the knowledge of the living God. I pray that the eyes of my understanding will be enlightened; that I may know what is the hope of His calling, what are the riches of the glory of His inheritance in the saints, and what is the exceeding greatness of His power towards us who believe, according to the working of His mighty power (Ephesians 1:17-18).
>
> Thank you Father for opening my eyes to see and my ears to hear what the Spirit of the Lord is saying and doing on the face of the earth today. Give me the courage and boldness to be able to say with the prophet Isaiah, "Here I am! Send me" (Isaiah 6:9). I will go where you direct me to go. I will do what you tell me to do. I will be a witness for you. I will share more, give more and pray more. I say, Yes Lord Jesus, use me in this final hour for your glory. Amen!

Instructions for a Daniel Fast

There are many different kinds of fasts mentioned in this book, but one of the most common is what we call a Daniel Fast. A Daniel Fast is a time to live and eat simply, and to consecrate yourself to the Lord. It is a time to seek the Lord and focus on His plan for the New Year.

There are several types of fasts seen in the book of Daniel. The first is found in Chapter 1. Daniel and his friends chose to refrain from the king's delicacies. This ten day selected food fast proves that God's way is better than man's way. Daniel and his friends found favor and increased in knowledge and influence because of this time of consecration.

Another fast in the Book of Daniel is found in Chapter 10, where it says, *"In those days I, Daniel, was mourning three full weeks. I ate no pleasant food, no meat or wine came into my mouth till three full weeks were fulfilled."* In other words, Daniel committed himself to **an extended partial fast for the purpose of seeking God about His will and purposes**.

The spiritual dynamics of what took place through this kind of consecration and prayer is found in Daniel 10:12-13, where we are given insights into human involvement in spiritual warfare. **Michael, the angel of Israel, defeated the "Prince of Persia"—the spiritual force that controlled Persia.**

The practical result of Daniel's fast is recorded in the book of Ezra, Chapter 1. We see that *"the Lord stirred up the spirit"* of a pagan King to allow the Jews to come out of captivity, and this king actually helped to pay for rebuilding the Temple in Jerusalem. This is one of the greatest historical miracles recorded in the Bible, and it happened because of intercessory prayer and fasting.

Instructions:

Choose your fast:

a) Media fast - no TV and/or radio, etc.
b) Pleasant food fast - no meats and no sweets
c) Meal fast - skip certain meals each week
d) Other - as the Lord directs you.

NOTE: Whatever is specifically chosen in terms of what you fast from, it is important that you also positively include a specific and special commitment to prayer beyond your usual prayer life.

Items to Pray Over

In this New Year, the Lord has a purpose that He desires to release upon you personally, upon your family, upon His Church and upon our nation. The following is an outline of some of the areas that you may desire to pray over in terms of spiritual breakthrough and Victory.

Personal Life:

a) Freedom from habits, addictions, and negative life-styles
b) For clear vision and direction from the Lord
c) For renewing and strengthening of relationship with the Lord
d) Other: ______________________________

Family Life:

a) Renewal of covenant and unity in the home
b) Household salvation(s)
c) The will and purposes of God for each member of your family
d) Peace, prosperity, health, and protection
e) Other: ______________________________

Church Life:

a) Unity and strengthening of relationships
b) Direction and Vision for the New Year:
   - Spirit of Revival and Renewal — Isa 58:6-12
   - Spiritual Freedom and Holiness — Isa. 61:11
   - Increase and Expansion — Isa. 60:1-5
   - Evangelism and salvation of souls — Acts 9:31
c) Specific needs
   - The pastoral staff and leadership
   - Ministry and financial resources
   - A Church Building
d) Life Groups, Outreach, Missions, Church Planting

Our Nation:

a) Pray for the leaders of our nation
b) Pray for revival over our nation — Ps. 72:8
c) Pray that we would be a blessing to the nations — Rev. 22:2
d) Other: ______________________________

Key: Find Scriptures to use in prayer as a basis of direction from God and as a weapon of authority against the enemy. Pastor Hazel Hill's book, "Praying God's Word" is an excellent resource.

20 Fasting Tips to Help you Succeed

The following are some common-sense suggestions on how to make your fasting adventure a little easier. One to three day fasts are common disciplines among many Christians. If you are healthy, they are generally medically safe, and can provide both physical and spiritual benefits. Remember, fasting is always voluntary, and a personal decision. If you are being treated for a medical condition, please be sure to check with your doctor first.

1. Drink lots of fluids. Keep them on hand, and in the refrigerator.
2. Prepare for each fast by eating lightly the day before you begin. Your tendency may be to gorge because of a fear of hunger. This will actually contribute to your system feeling even more deprived.
3. Develop a strategy to avoid food shopping and meal preparation for others. Pre-prepared meals that can be heated as needed, plenty of sandwich fixin's, and of course, frozen dinners work well.
4. If you are being treated for a medical condition, please consult your doctor first. Also, pregnant women and diabetics should not fast. When conditions prevent a complete fast, please consider a "Daniel" fast. (Daniel fast is fasting your favorite foods and maintaining on bland or simple foods.)
5. Plan to be busy during your fast, rather than sitting around thinking about your empty stomach. At normal meal times, study your Bible and pray, even at work.

"Snack" on the Bible frequently for special verses you can meditate on.

6. Pray in the Spirit often, whenever there is opportunity.
7. If fasting a full day and skipping supper, plan for early bedtime to avoid the late evening munchies.
8. If you experience a period of weakness, try fruit juice to get a little sugar into your system.
9. Don't watch TV food commercials. They know what it takes to hook you.
10. Apply spiritual authority to your body when it begins to "talk back." Remember that the real you is the person on the inside - your spirit. Your body is your servant. Take authority over it and tell it who is in charge, just as you would if it was being tempted to sin.
11. Call a pastor or spiritual friend for assurance and encouragement.
12. Study fasting in the Bible and in Christian books on the subject. Education on a subject strengthens our resolve, and sharpens our focus.
13. Bear in mind that short term fasting is both safe and satisfying, and has been endorsed by various medical and health experts as being beneficial in many ways. If you are healthy and drinking plenty of fluids, you are not in any danger. Like most Americans, you are just unaccustomed to being hungry. It is similar to your first trip to the gym after you have decided to shape up. Because you are not used to strenuous exercise, the next day your body will complain. In both cases, "no pain, no gain."
14. Speaking of exercise, try to limit strenuous activities that will deplete the body of fluids during a fast. Moderate exercise is okay, but watch the heat.
15. Focus on the fact that the Head of our church, Jesus

Christ, has led the way in fasting (40 days on one occasion), and has asked us to follow His example. God's Son would never lead us to harm, but only to abundant living (John 10:10).

16. When breaking a fast, don't overeat or you will pay the price. Let your first meal be a light one, and then snack a little later if still hungry. On fasts of three or more days, your digestive system has slowed down, and is on stand-by. It will take a day or so for it to cycle back to normal.

17. Headaches can occur when fasting due to the purging of toxins that have been stored in your system. They are now being released as a part of the "back-up" energy source. Pray, continue to drink plenty of fluids to flush your system, and feel free to take over-the-counter medication such as aspirin or acetaminophen, if needed.

18. Nausea can occur if you take certain medications on an empty stomach, such as antibiotics. This is also true of some vitamins. Some people find water helps settle the stomach. Others may prefer a little milk or clear soup broth in advance of taking medication to calm the stomach.

19. If you reach a point to where you are about to give up your fast before you wanted to, try a liquid meal drink. This can often take the edge off enough to keep you going.

20. If you totally blow it, do not get under condemnation. Successful fasting must be learned. God still loves us, and our effort means more to God than not trying at all. Determine at the point of caving-in that you will live to fast another day. You will find success, one meal, and one day at a time. God bless you.

Other Resources by Drs. George and Hazel Hill

If you enjoyed Fasting for Breakthrough and Revival, you will be equally blessed by these other dynamic books and CDs.

Praying God's Word
Book $12.00

Praying God's Word
CD $15.00

Covenant Relationships
Book $11.95

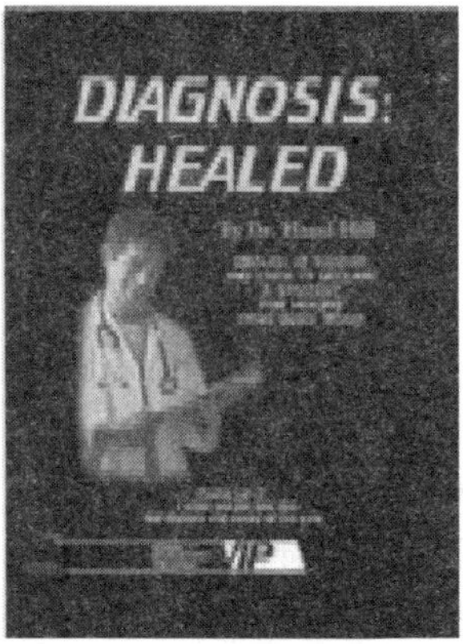

Diagnosis: Healed CD and Booklet $15.00

Notes

Notes

Notes

Notes

Notes

Notes